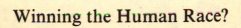

Winning the Human Race?

Winning the Human Race?

The Report of the Independent Commission on International Humanitarian Issues

Foreword by
Sadruddin Aga Khan and Hassan bin Talal

Zed Books Ltd
London and New Jersey

Winning the Human Race? was first published by Zed Books Ltd.,
57 Caledonian Road, London N1 9BU and
171 First Avenue, Atlantic Highlands, New Jersey 07716, in 1988.

Cover design by Andrew Corbett
Typeset by EMS Photosetters, Rochford, Essex
Printed and bound in Great Britain by Cox and Wyman Ltd., Reading

British Library Cataloguing in Publication Data

Winning the human race? The report of
the Independent Commission on International
Humanitarian Issues.
1. Human rights
I. Independent Commission on International
Humanitarian Issues
323.4

ISBN 0-86232-800-4
ISBN 0-86232-801-2 Pbk

Contents

PART II: THE VICTIMS

PART III: THE HOPE

ANNEXES 200

The Independent Commission on International Humanitarian Issues

Co-Chairmen
Sadruddin Aga Khan (Iran)   Hassan bin Talal (Jordan)

Members
Susanna Agnelli   (Italy)
Talal Bin Abdul Aziz Al Saud (Saudi Arabia)
Paulo Evaristo Arns   (Brazil)
Mohammed Bedjaoui   (Algeria)
Henrik Beer   (Sweden)
Igor Blishchenko   (USSR)
Luis Echeverria Alvarez   (Mexico)
Pierre Graber   (Switzerland)
Ivan Head   (Canada)
M. Hidayatullah   (India)
Aziza Hussein   (Egypt)
Manfred Lachs   (Poland)
Robert McNamara   (USA)
Lazar Mojsov   (Yugoslavia)
Mohamed Mzali   (Tunisia)
Sadako Ogata   (Japan)
David Owen   (United Kingdom)
Willibald P. Pahr   (Austria)
Shridath S. Ramphal   (Guyana)
Ru Xin   (China)
Salim A. Salim   (Tanzania)
Léopold Sédar Senghor   (Senegal)
Soedjatmoko   (Indonesia)
Desmond Tutu   (South Africa)
Simone Veil   (France)
Gough Whitlam   (Australia)

Secretary General, ex-officio member:
Zia Rizvi   (Pakistan)

Foreword

The title of this Report highlights the question our Commission set out to explore. The human race is engaged in a race against time. It is not just the quality of life, but life itself, that is threatened. Modern man is at peace neither with himself nor his environment. And yet never before in history have humans wielded as much power over their destiny and their planet. To avoid becoming victims of their own ingenuity, they must now ensure that wisdom and foresight prevail over knowledge and technological advances.

As this turbulent century draws to its end, humankind is poised at a crossroads: in one direction lies self-annihilation, in the other the possibility of unprecedented prosperity for all. Winning the human race is the challenge faced by contemporary society. It cannot be met in our view without placing human welfare at the centre of national and international policy-making.

Our Commission came into being in response to the urgently felt need to bring to humanitarian concerns the same level of experience and expertise as is usually accorded to economic and security matters. There is a growing awareness that economic growth is only worthwhile if it is accompanied by adequate social development. Our purpose was neither to embark upon a philosophical enquiry into the human condition nor to plead for idealism. Rather, it was to identify realistic options for action regarding specific humanitarian problems which, in our opinion, were not being adequately addressed. We wished also to make the poor and the powerless visible and audible, to plead for unity in diversity and to articulate a humanitarian perspective to cope with the vicissitudes of an increasingly complex global society.

We recognized at the outset that in order to encourage action we need to enhance public awareness. Hence this Report and, indeed, the series of sectoral reports on a variety of humanitarian issues which have been published under the auspices of our Commission. In view of the encouraging response from the general public and governments, particularly in the developing countries, these reports have within a short time become available in many editions and languages.

We are fully aware that a report is not, and should not be, an end in itself but just one of the means to encourage appropriate action. During the limited life-span of the Commission, we were able to publish our findings on only a few of the issues we examined. Information on these, and on the series of documentary films which complement the published reports, is contained in an annex to this book. The role of our Commission has therefore been a limited one in comparison to the ever-increasing humanitarian problems faced by the international community. We hope and trust that it will nonetheless act as a catalyst in heightening awareness and encouraging action.

We are gratified that a number of tangible results have already emerged from our recommendations and suggestions regarding specific issues. Governments and international organizations have taken measures ranging from improvement of early warning systems and disaster management, to action on behalf of vulnerable groups such as street children, displaced and stateless persons and indigenous peoples. Many governments have responded to our appeal to adhere to the instruments of international humanitarian law and to alleviate unnecessary suffering caused by armed conflicts. In our view, the process begun four decades ago with the Universal Declaration of Human Rights, and built upon by a number of conventions since then, ought to be further strengthened by a Declaration of Humanitarian Principles in order to guide policies and actions at global level.

To ensure an active follow-up to our Report, we decided to

encourage the establishment of an Independent Bureau for Humanitarian Issues for a limited period of time. The United Nations General Assembly took note of this in its Resolution 42/120 of 7 December 1987 relating to the work of our Commission. The Bureau will have the task of disseminating the message of the Commission and of serving as a bridge between reflection and action. Building upon the results already obtained, it will help promote global consensus based on common ethical values. Action-oriented and practical in its approach, it will concentrate essentially on specific humanitarian problems which are likely to arise or get worse in the future.

We are deeply appreciative of the assistance and goodwill afforded us by countless individuals and organizations. In particular, we wish to express our profound gratitude to our fellow Commissioners who generously gave so much of their time and energy to this common endeavour. Their individual contributions as members of various Working Groups of the Commission are acknowledged in the sectoral reports. In the preparation of this Report, we wish to thank our colleagues: Soedjatmoko for his valuable contribution to the first chapter, Shridath Ramphal for chapters two and three and Robert McNamara and David Owen for chapter four. The remaining chapters are a synthesis of our common deliberations in the Working Groups and plenary sessions. Zia Rizvi, in addition to heading the Secretariat of the Commission, acted as the co-ordinating editor of the sectoral reports and assumed the overall responsibility for the editing of this Report. To him and his colleagues in the Secretariat, as well as the innumerable experts and consultants from all parts of the world enumerated in one of the annexes to the Report, we wish to record our deepest appreciation and warmest thanks. The active interest taken by the Secretary-General of the United Nations and the contributions made by various governmental and non-governmental agencies are gratefully acknowledged.

In commending this Report to the attention of the public and policy-makers alike, we wish to reaffirm our faith in human destiny. Ours is a message of hope. But to nurture it, neither noble intentions nor fine words will suffice. Action inspired by goodwill is called for. In the context of the new humanitarian

Winning the Human Race?

order which the United Nations is instrumental in promoting, we hope the process begun by us will be sustained and invigorated.

Hassan bin Talal   **Sadruddin Aga Khan**

Co-Chairmen

PART I
THE CHALLENGE

1. The Ethics of Human Solidarity

"If the universe is non-ethical by our present standards, we must reconsider those standards and reconstruct our ethics."

H. G. Wells, 1901

Humanitarianism is a basic orientation towards the interests and welfare of people. It demands that whatever detracts from human well-being must be questioned, regardless of its effects on economic growth, political power, or the stability of a certain order. Abstractions such as growth, stability and order are not ends in themselves, but have value only if they bring about the greater welfare of people.

Humanitarianism proceeds from the recognition that each one of us is no more but also no less than a human being. To emphasize our common humanity is not to deny or play down the importance of transcendental concerns, but simply to recognize that no single definition of truth is universally and unconditionally accepted. Common humanity is a point we can start with, as we learn to live with multiple perceptions of the truth.

The humanitarian perspective takes a long-range view of human welfare, and one of its essential dimensions is solidarity with future generations. Our first responsibility to our children is to ensure that they have a future by avoiding catastrophic war. It is also necessary to ensure that they do not inherit a planet whose environment has been substantially diminished or irreparably destroyed. We have a responsibility not to deprive our descendants of the chance to live fully and to push forward the frontiers of knowledge for the benefit of humankind. We have an obligation not to foreclose the options available to them. Humanitarianism is cautious. It has a strong bias against the irreversible.

We uphold humanitarianism as a framework for recognizing

3

dilemmas and a formula for resolving them. Once human welfare has been placed firmly at the centre of individual and collective concerns, however, there are still a host of questions to be resolved in any specific set of circumstances. The humanitarian perspective includes an ethical orientation that equips us to approach these difficult questions: **an ethic of human solidarity**.

The identification of common values from which to construct an ethical framework for human solidarity is dependent upon the establishment of a broader consensus about the meaning of humanitarianism, and about its role in the promotion of human welfare.

For us, humanitarianism is both an attitude for individuals and a framework for policy-makers. It encompasses both humanism and human rights and goes beyond the confines of existing humanitarian law. It connects ethics to action at all levels. In this sense, we attribute to the term humanitarianism a broader context than its current usage permits.

Traditional concepts of humanitarianism tend to be negative in character, concerned more with refraining from certain actions which harm others than actually helping. They remain limited in scope. Providing emergency solutions to urgent social problems is, of course, a first priority, but too often they have come to be used as a substitute for addressing the root causes and providing long-term answers.

A more universal moral perspective suits our times, because we are linked so much more closely to one another. An expansion of humanitarianism better to match modern needs must occur in several dimensions: horizontal, to cover more of the globe and include a multitude of actors; vertical, to take in new kinds of moral issues; and temporal, to cover future generations. And there must be an accompanying reform of individual, collective and institutional attitudes to accommodate this expansion.

The Challenge

In a world of shrinking spaces, porous national boundaries, expanding technological capacity and instant communication, we live in an imperfect but vivid relationship with all of our fellow human-beings. Our attention to any one segment of humanity may be limited or self-limiting. But our mutual ability to affect each other's lives, for better or for worse, has never had the scope and immediacy that it has today.

Modern communications have played an important role in strengthening our sense of human solidarity. This was seen most recently and dramatically when the images and descriptions of the famine in Africa burst upon the consciousness of the public everywhere in the world. Coming face-to-face, in an almost literal sense, with suffering on such a scale challenges people's notions of what it means to be human. It brings about an expansion of our moral universe.

Many kinds of environmental problems, such as air pollution, acid rain or the effects of destructive land-use practices, do not respect international borders. Increasingly refugees, other displaced people or migrant workers are also crossing national borders in large numbers. The vast population movements that are now taking place give rise to a plethora of humanitarian problems. Those who are obliged to leave their homes often become targets of exploitation, discrimination or debilitating dependency; those who remain behind often face inhumane conditions.

Man's inhumanity to man is not an invention of the modern era, but the scope and scale of his capacity to act it out is historically unprecedented. Age-old themes such as greed, betrayal of popular will, lust for power and ethnic hatred combine with contemporary economic and social strains to create new sources of conflict. Rivalry over land and resources has intensified, spurred by the need to satisfy the requirements and aspirations of increasing populations.

The greatest obstacle to the achievement of a sense of community based on an inclusive ethical consensus is the drifting apart of the rich and the poor into two separate worlds. Today, this is a far more complex phenomenon than the geopolitical division of the world into North and South or industrialized and developing countries. The rich in the capitals of the Third World have far more in common with the rich of the First World than they have with the poor in their own countries. The affluent also communicate more easily with each

5

other across national boundaries than with their poor compatriots. Technologies of communication and transportation, to say nothing of a pervasive consumerist culture, have helped to create a new stratification of the world's people into transnational classes that share very little information, experience or common concern with others. The gap in understanding between rich and poor is in imminent danger of reaching the point where the only form of discourse may be violent conflict, occasionally punctuated by outbursts of charity. It is matter of the greatest practical, as well as ethical urgency, to prevent the split between the two worlds from widening, and to restore a sense of solidarity among people.

The human person in today's world is particularly vulnerable. For millions of people, violence has become a fact of life. Wars continue to plague developing countries. Civilian casualties have greatly risen in proportion to combatant casualties. In scores of countries, torture is becoming institutionalized as an instrument of state control and repression. Weapons of indiscriminate destruction are being used increasingly in armed conflicts while nuclear weapons have become the sword of Damocles of modern times. Starvation continues to be used as a means of suppressing opposition, while control over civilian populations serves as a tactic as well as an objective of armed conflict.

Scientific and technological developments have given human-beings powers that far outstrip their collective good judgement. Formidable conventional weapons are easily available, even to small groups. Consequently, every country with an aggrieved minority, faces a potential risk. With the development of modern weapons of mass destruction, the power of the instruments of war has reached levels never before imagined, so that even those States not directly involved in a conflict have a strong interest in helping to resolve it. In today's volatile world, conflicts cannot easily be contained and isolated. Furthermore, each time a violation of international law is tolerated, it sets a dangerous precedent that makes it more likely that similar abuses will be repeated.

The State is on the defensive. The pursuit of national security has come to place excessive reliance on the threatened use of force. This has led to the militarization of whole societies to the detriment of the economic, social and political sectors. State authorities seem to be increasingly willing to use violence, not only in their relations with other States but also against their own people.

In some cases, this turmoil may be a part of the struggle to throw off the remnants of colonial structures and power relationships. But in many more, the end of the colonial era has been followed by periods of contention and unrest as mechanisms for political representation failed to take hold. Even without the wilful appropriation of state power, the development process itself generates inequalities that a representative government must mediate. All too often, however, States have failed in, or abandoned, their mediating roles and substituted repression for social management.

With all societies so vulnerable to the actions of others, and all faced with the possibility of extinction, the need to formulate new standards for humanitarian decision-making is imperative. General rules and principles of human conduct have evolved and acquired authority in specific historical settings. But in a shrinking world and in a situation of rapid social, economic and technological change, it is necessary to find common values that are acceptable across a wide spectrum of cultures and ideologies.

Increasingly, ambivalence and uncertainty characterize the ethical choices that people are called upon to make. These arise because worthy goals can and do conflict with each other, because contemporary life puts before us a multiplicity of choices and because we cannot perfectly foresee or control all the consequences of our actions. In any complex situation, the unintended consequences of a choice may overwhelm the intended result. Even with an ethical orientation toward human well-being, we cannot, everywhere and at all times, completely eliminate risk or catastrophe. Nor is it always possible to prevent people from doing what they believe to be right even if the price in terms of human suffering, death and desolation, is very high.

The Framework

Certain ethical imperatives follow from the fact that we cannot control and predict the consequences of our actions in a complex environment. They include:

* The responsibility to examine and attempt to understand the full range of consequences of an action and avoid one-dimensional thinking.

* To make every effort to minimize harm and to compensate the sufferers when harm is unavoidably generated in pursuit of a competing good.

* To exercise discernment in the face of unintended consequences or harm. Justifiable actions may hurt some people. However it is important to acknowledge any ill effects for what they are rather than insisting that they are acceptable because they cannot be avoided.

Inaction can be as decisive as action, and just as damaging. On the other hand, the need to act without full knowledge or total certainty is a major dilemma for those who hold power. The fact is that no single person or institution has the capacity to marshall all the facts, understand all the alternatives, or predict all the reactions to and interpretations of an action. This underscores the crucial importance of continual discourse on ethical issues. Exposure to different ways of looking at a problem may, therefore, increase understanding and in so doing enlarge areas of agreement. This is a necessary first step for an expanded consensus on humanitarian issues.

Such a consensus must necessarily take into account the increasing prominence of new actors, particularly in recent decades, both within and outside the governmental structures of new States or States that have radically changed their political system. However, these new actors have emerged from nations, cultures and ideologies that did not participate in formulating the international consensus on humanitarian norms, and have not had the opportunity to give their views on it. It is not surprising that they feel little obligation to abide by it.

Many of the new States do not have adequate experience of national politics, much less of international politics. Moreover, many States that accept international standards in external conflicts still refuse to apply humanitarian norms to the internal ones when dealing with opposition groups. These groups thus lack the incentive of mutual restraint to apply the norms themselves.

One additional explanatory factor in the fragility of the humanitarian consensus may be that the consensus itself has not drawn sufficiently upon non-Western cultural, legal and religious traditions. The historical reasons for this are clear. The norms of humanitarian conduct, therefore, might become more universally acceptable if they draw on more universal, rather than strictly Western sources of inspiration. The holy texts of various religions and the legal systems, philosophies, and customary practices of other cultures, including oral traditions, abound in moral injunctions that imply an ethic of human solidarity.

The international community can condemn violations of humanitarian standards but it can hardly claim to be surprised when desperate people react violently, and in so doing disregard basic humanitarian principles. The first reaction of the perpetrators to pleas for restraint is likely to be: 'Where was the outrage of the international community, whose norms we are now being asked to respect, during the crises that imprisoned us in poverty, ignorance and oppression, that killed our children through malnutrition and disease, that despoiled our lands?' The keen sense of structural violence on the part of its victims, and their determination to resist it, is the link that joins long-term issues of poverty and injustice to the breakdown of humanitarian norms in wars or violent internal struggles. The contenders in such struggles are not likely to observe the norms set by the international community until they are acknowledged to be a part of it themselves.

Dual standards, or multiple standards tailored to specific circumstances or to the perceptions and ideologies of separate societies are a luxury that can no longer be afforded. International standards must be such as to be acceptable across a wide spectrum of cultures and ideologies. They must be based on the notion of the human species as a single, indivisible but pluralistic unit.

The tenuousness of human judgement is an inescapable fact of life. However, to reduce the margin for error, we must strive to keep the channels of communication with others open. The

9

broadest possible discourse can at the very least uncover differences of conviction and their sources. Exposure to different ways of looking at a problem may increase understanding and in so doing enlarge areas of agreement. Sometimes, received opinion may be false, or it may be necessary to clear up apprehensions about erroneous opinion. But the commoner case than either of these, is when conflicting opinions, instead of being one true and the other false, share the truth between them, and an exchange takes place to supply the remainder of the truth.

Calls for a strong international consensus are often dismissed as unattainable, for they raise fears of forced imposition of a uniform system of values on a highly pluralistic world. Such uniformity is neither necessary nor desirable, for an international consensus can and should be a minimum one. It requires identifying a few irreducible values – but these may have a different configuration among themselves and in relation to other values, depending on their cultural setting. What is important is not the configuration, but rather that within each culturally specific setting the irreducible values are to be found. Each nation has a stake in helping to identify the core of the humanitarian ethic, and in tolerating many different expressions of it.

For centuries, the great religious texts have taught the essential oneness of the human race. That transcendent perception of common humanity seems to have waned, though it may yet be reawakened. It is strongly buttressed by the facts of mutual reliance as well as the logic of moral philosophy and it is fully consistent with the reality of international pluralism. Living together on this plant with its finite resources, where we all have the ability to hurt if not destroy each other, requires an enlargement of our vision and sense of neighbourhood.

Neighbours are bound together in mutual reliance, and in that sense all people today surely qualify as neighbours. But we lack the positive qualities of neighbourliness: **an acknowledgment of mutual obligation, and a reasonable level of tolerance**. It may be that the classic neighbourhood is also a place of intense suspicion, jealousy and even hostility. But its members know that they must live together, and that the expression of open antagonism leaves them all poorer and less secure. There is also a degree of acceptance, within bounds, of the faults of one's neighbours on the grounds that they display a weakness that we may all have to some degree. In the final analysis, they too belong despite what we may not like in them.

What we need is an explanation and justification of moral obligations which are predicated upon ensuring mutual welfare. It is natural to talk about helping those with whom we are in immediate contact, but here we are talking about those far away as well. The duty to help those in need, at least within the family circle and the immediate community if not the nation and the world, is widely if not universally acknowledged in some form. Psychologically, most human-beings are made uncomfortable by the suffering of others. But why should one be concerned with persons one does not even know?

In part the answer lies in the combined notions of **solidarity** and **reciprocity**. The main motivation in the present times comes from the increasing realization that adversity anywhere is a threat to prosperity everywhere. Solidarity and reciprocity thus take the form of **enlightened self-interest**. This is based on the realization that inequalities which are incompatible with human dignity are politically, socially and economically destabilizing. The willingness to ignore humanitarian needs is likely to encourage the same attitude in others.

General rules and principles of human conduct have evolved in specific historical settings, and within those settings they have acquired strong presumptive authority. But in a situation of rapid social, cultural and technological change, the old principles may lose their acceptability as ethical guidelines. Still, it is possible to define the outer limits of ethical behaviour that would be acceptable very widely in the modern world. What is more difficult to define is ethical decision-making within those limits, in the complex, ambiguous, uncertain and fast-changing circumstances in which humanitarian issues unfold.

It must be recognized that the problem is not of morality versus politics but rather of the kind of politics which allow moral restraints to emerge and to be observed. Such political activity begins with a sober consideration of the underlying self-interest that will persuade States and other actors to accept the precepts of common humanity.

The willingness to blunt voluntarily the sharper edges of national sovereignty can be seen in all successful efforts to bring about greater international co-operation. It is essential to the task of preserving and extending humanitarian values. Restraint in the exercise of sovereignty does not require an undermining or superseding of the State. It does, however, imply the need to agree upon effective and mutually agreed methods for holding States accountable for their actions, or for their inaction, in the face of another's dereliction of humanitarian obligations.

We recognize that disregard for humanitarian values is not found only in situations of overt conflict. It is also manifest in the willingness of the international community to stand by while hundreds of millions of people sink into the depths of absolute deprivation. This amounts to acceptance of a doctrine of dispensability applicable to the poorest and most helpless members of society. While the first line of responsibility for them rests with their own communities and States, these are often helpless to remedy a harmful situation. Often, they lack the resources or the skills to combat deprivation, or are in the grip of larger forces in the national or the world economy over which they have no control.

A broader consensus on humanitarian issues requires, in our view, a search for the highest common values that are widely shared despite all the negative, conflictual elements of human societies. All cultures and religions credit human-beings with a moral dimension and expect to see it manifested in however fragmented and diluted a form.

The conceptual framework within which our Commission functioned was based essentially on an ethical core which can help build a wider consensus. The cornerstones of this framework were the values which from time immemorial have been a part of the collective consciousness of the human species, which have ensured their survival and well-being, and which have stood the test of time:

* Respect for life;
* A responsibility towards future generations;
* Protection of the human habitat;

* Altruism nurtured by a sense of mutual interest and a recognition of human dignity and worth.

We have borne in mind these values when examining the specific humanitarian issues which form the bulk of this Report. Recognizing the value of a pragmatic and realistic approach, we endeavoured at the same time to remain fully conscious of the over-arching global issues which condition the humanitarian problems as well as the new forces which are bound to affect, for better or for worse, the future shape of things. These are treated briefly in the first part of our Report.

Our purpose was no more than to be catalytic, however modestly, in encouraging public debate on the need for people to be more humane in facing contemporary challenges. We are fully aware that the idea of human solidarity and the ethics which must cement it imply an almost Copernican change of perspective, from a fractured to a holistic view of human welfare which is centred on the commonality of human interests. The task of building a consensus around an ethic of human solidarity is a long-term proposition. The key is to engage individuals in collective action at all levels: to bring the needy to see themselves as individuals whose primary purpose is self-sufficiency; and to bring to those in a position to help, the understanding that true self-realization involves the alleviation of others' suffering. Progress in removing the causes of human suffering is a step-by-step proposition which calls for tenacious efforts on a long-term basis. This should not be a source of discouragement, but rather accepted as a challenge that the eternal human spirit needs to achieve its own fulfilment.

2. Global Issues

"I believe that man will not merely endure. He will prevail."

William Faulkner, 1950

The astronauts' vision of our small and fragile planet confirmed for the first time through the human eye what the mind had long known and what the manifold interconnections of human activity across the globe daily demonstrate: the nations of the world are inseparably linked. It is generally recognized that global issues can only be dealt with multilaterally, through the combined action of governments, international and regional organizations and, probably most important of all, the peoples immediately affected. However, global problems do not necessarily have global solutions. Every region and every culture has its own specificity. While some of today's most pressing problems – the population explosion, the deteriorating environment, the growing poverty in the Third World, the proliferation of mass destruction weapons, terrorism and drug abuse – require the co-operation of governments as well as a multitude of institutions and individuals across the world, their particular solutions may call for differing treatment. A humanitarian response to the great issues of our time recognizes both their global nature and the need for flexibility in approach.

In order to avoid duplication with the work of existing organizations at national and international level on the global issues dealt with in this chapter and in view of the limited mandate and time available to our Commission, we did not examine these issues in depth. However, for the purpose of highlighting their humanitarian implications and with a view to presenting a comprehensive picture of the human condition, we felt it would be useful to flag some of the global issues of relevance to our work. The following paragraphs of our Report should be viewed in that light.

Population

Few contemporary issues have as far-reaching humanitarian implications as the problem of world population growth. At the beginning of this century, our planet had less than two billion people. Today it supports over five billion and is expected to sustain over six billion by the end of the century. Although the world's population increases by more than a million every five days, the rate of increase is slowly diminishing. However, the decline in the rate of world population growth is distorted and deceptive. The fall has occurred almost exclusively in China and the developed countries. Ironically, birth rates remain high in countries which can least afford big populations. As mortality rates continue to come down and the number of women entering childbearing age grows, the world population is expected steadily to increase to almost ten billion before it stabilizes.

The pattern of world population growth, which has important humanitarian implications, is likely to remain uneven. According to the United Nations, more than 90 per cent of the expected increase between 1980 and 2025 will be concentrated in developing countries. The greatest expansion is projected to be in Africa whose 1980 population of 476 million is expected to more than triple by 2025. By then the populations of Latin America and South Asia are expected to have almost doubled, that of East Asia to have increased by 43 per cent, those of North America and the Soviet Union to have grown by 38 per cent, but that of Europe by only 9 per cent. By the year 2025, 83 per cent of the world's population will be living in Asia, Africa and Latin America.

The already difficult task of national development is being made increasingly arduous for many countries by continuing high rates of population growth. This is bound to exacerbate further existing economic and social strains.

The prospect of future population growth will inevitably coincide with changing age structures heavily weighted towards the young in developing countries. In some, as much as 50 per

15

cent of the total population is already under 15 years of age, compared to about 20 per cent in developed countries. By the end of the century, the population under 30 years old will increase by over 500 million in developing countries and constitute 60 per cent of the population.

The increasing number of young people, especially in developing countries, has made it considerably more difficult to meet their basic needs. Although many children engage in economically productive work in the developing world, a relatively small percentage of the adult population bears primary responsibility for feeding, clothing, housing and educating them. As a result, millions of children, the most vulnerable segment of the global community, are neglected, abandoned and forced to fend for themselves.

But the problems are not all likely to occur with the burgeoning number of young people. As health care improves and mortality rates decline, the number of elderly people (age 65 and over) continues to grow. By the end of the century, the world's elderly population will increase by 43 per cent. Over 70 per cent of this increase will occur in developing countries. Although the elderly will account for only 5 per cent and 13 per cent of the developing and developed countries' populations respectively, there is an emerging fear that the cost of caring for the elderly will become overly burdensome. Traditional support for the unique social, economic and medical needs of the aged has already begun to erode, as struggling young populations place greater demands on relatively limited resources. Unless comprehensive forward-looking programmes are designed and implemented to enable the elderly to be independent and productive in their latter years, this clash of priorities will only worsen. Moreover, in the developed countries, the quality of life and medical care have ensured longevity. At the same time, the population growth of many of these countries is stagnant. Caring for the aged is bound to strain the welfare state, engendering new humanitarian problems. While populations in the North will be ageing, the populations in the South will be getting younger. This imbalance will have its own repercussions on North/South relations.

In order to introduce some balance in the uncontrolled

growth in the population of developing countries, programmes to encourage greater use of family planning seem not only desirable but essential, as the countries most seriously affected have themselves acknowledged. However, it is important that these programmes only take place with the agreement and co-operation of the individuals involved. Greater emphasis on education and training about family planning is required. Moreover, there is now a general recognition that poverty is a prime cause as well as an effect of excessive population growth. Poor people tend to have larger families as a form of socio-economic insurance. Population policies must therefore go hand in hand with development programmes designed to raise the incomes of the poor, literacy levels and the status of women.

One specific aspect of the disparities in wealth and population increases between the North and the South is the increasing movement of populations from the poor countries to the rich. Although the numbers of people moving to the North is relatively small, they are already straining the absorption capacity of the receiving countries. This, in turn, is leading to the emergence of xenophobia and increased social tensions. This phenomenon needs to be studied not only in terms of national economies and labour markets but also in the context of its social and humanitarian implications. Above all, there is a need to address the root causes of these population movements and to develop imaginative long-term policies which fully take into account the humanitarian aspects.

The problems of over-population and rapid population increase are largely being left for future generations to tackle. Many parts of the world are faced with the continuing prospect as well as already existing reality of widespread hunger and poverty, massive unemployment, rapid urban growth and environmental degradation.

Although more food is being produced globally than ever before, more people are chronically malnourished than at any previous time. Yet it is estimated that our planet possesses enough food, minerals and energy resources to sustain life at an adequate level for at least 10 billion people – twice the present world population.

Environment

The rapid growth of the world's population is also causing damage to the environment. Among the ecological stresses associated with overpopulation are overgrazing, depleting fish stocks, deforestation, soil erosion, desertification and the loss of unique species. Over one-third of the world's arable land is threatened by desertification, a subject dealt with later in this Report. The demand for water is growing at a greater rate than the world's population due to expanding agricultural, industrial and domestic use. In the near future, water shortages are expected to become increasingly frequent, particularly in urban areas.

Efforts are called for to contain erosion, increase water retention and replant forests in order to meet estimated needs by the end of the century. Conservation measures, long-term planning and adequate allocation of resources are necessary. Grave damage to the earth's life-support system has already occurred and will escalate unless well-planned measures are taken. However, governmental responses to date have been disappointing.

Damage to the environment occurs not only because too many people are concentrated in a given location but also because they are struggling to survive. A substantial amount of environmental destruction takes place out of sheer human necessity coupled with ignorance. That ignorance is not only the property of those people living and struggling to survive at the very margins of existence. Damage has also been inflicted on the environment by industrialized societies which have tended to ignore the ecological consequences of their actions. In the long term, the result affects us all, rich and poor alike.

Atmospheric pollution caused by the use of fossil fuels, the clearing and burning of forests, and intensive agricultural practices involving pesticides and other synthetic chemicals, threatens to harm the environment irreparably. Scientists estimate that a build-up in the atmosphere of certain carbon, nitrogen and chlorine compounds will change the earth's climate more during the next 50 to 75 years than has happened over the last 15,000 years – the so-called greenhouse effect. Scientists are also increasingly expressing concern about the depletion of the ozone layer due to extensive use of chlorofluorocarbons. Temperature and rainfall patterns may be affected worldwide, the level of the seas may rise and the earth's eco-systems be upset in unpredictable ways. The annual cost of such a climatic change could approach 3 per cent of the world's gross economic output, perhaps cancelling the benefits of economic growth.

Our abuse of the environment has now reached beyond the atmosphere to litter space with technological debris. Ultimately human-beings and the soil of their planet are one common clay. It would be tragic if global destruction, rather than attention to global needs or acceptance of global fellowship, were to bring that realization home.

We recognize that this brief account of environmental problems does not do justice to a subject which has important implications for us and for future generations. We direct attention to the detailed studies of the humanitarian aspects of desertification and deforestation which have been carried out by our Commission as well as the 1987 Report of the World Commission on Environment and Development.*

Poverty and Development

The elimination of poverty and the satisfaction of basic human needs is still a goal which challenges both individuals and societies. Indeed, despite all individual, national and international efforts, the majority of people encounter famine, disease and death as an almost daily consequence of their poverty. All our technological achievements and all our mastery of material things do not prevent human-beings from dying of malnutrition every minute of every day somewhere on this planet.

There remain large areas of absolute poverty, particularly in Africa and Asia. Far from improving, in Sub-Saharan Africa per capita incomes have been falling for over a decade. Low-income Africa is now poorer than in 1960, and the World Bank

---

* *Our Common Future*, Oxford University Press, 1987.

projects a further decline over the next decade. The prospects for the absolute poor, now numbering some 800 million, are more desperate than ever before.

This tragic situation cries out for remedy. Human development is the ultimate goal of national development. Yet, after four decades of developmental efforts by the international community, hundreds of millions of our fellow human-beings still live and die in hunger. Much of the reason why the development process is facing great strains and renewed uncertainty is to be found in the recent world recession. The international economy favours the rich industrialized countries. Indeed in recent years the world has moved away from international economic co-operation and may be moving towards a new era of economic domination and dependence.

At a time when the world is experiencing a great mobility of capital, the needy countries of the Third World are being starved of funds. The total net flow of money from the West to the Third World has fallen dramatically in the 1980s. The biggest falls have been in private investment, commercial bank loans and government export credits. The fall in private capital transfers, the largest part of total resource flows, has been particularly sharp, from $74 billion in 1981 to only $29 billion in 1985, with bank loans falling even further than investment. Aid from Western countries to the Third World has fallen to 0.35 per cent of gross domestic product, half of the target set by the United Nations in 1971 of 0.7 per cent.

As Third World populations grew by some 10 per cent between 1981 and 1985, total resource flows from Western countries per recipient actually fell by nearly 50 per cent. The developing countries need to double the present inflows of capital by 1990 if they are to achieve a growth rate of 5 per cent a year. Debt servicing now outstrips new financial flows to the Third World. In June 1986, the World Bank itself revealed that it had become a net recipient of funds from middle-income developing countries. Africa will be heavily dependent over the next few years on major external capital flows simply for recovery The need for fresh flows of capital to the poorer countries is greater than ever.

However, the concern of ordinary people, particularly in the industrialized countries has grown as that of their governments has diminished. In 1985, the year of worldwide publicity for the famine in Africa, the non-governmental organizations, which include the major famine relief agencies, recorded an impressive 20 per cent increase in their contributions. The overall picture, however, remains one of inadequacy in the face of ever-increasing human need.

The struggle against poverty is crucial to the future of our global human society and it concerns people and governments everywhere. There is a need to increase agricultural yields, as well as to make major policy changes in the relationship of agriculture to industry and of farmers to city dwellers. Some one billion people in rural areas of the Third World are landless or nearly so. Costly programmes of land reclamation, rural credit and infrastructural development are required and the problem of land distribution needs to be addressed.

Yet the necessary emphasis on agriculture must not obscure the needs of the world's city dwellers. At the present time our planet has some 250 cities of over a million people each. Of these 100 are in the developing world. By the end of the century there will be 440 such cities and 300 – almost two-thirds – of them will be in the developing world. Poverty, illiteracy, malnutrition, disease, high infant mortality and low life-expectancy, and the resultant denial of human potential for the multitude of individuals concerned will put severe strains on the social, national and international fabric of our society.

Global Militarization

Perhaps, for the first time in human history, millions of people the world over are not just uncertain about their own future or concerned about their children's future, they are deeply anxious about the future of our entire planet. Their anxiety springs from the fact that man now has the capacity to eradicate human life from this planet many times over. With the aid of their military industrial establishments, the superpowers have, during recent years, elevated their rivalry to such a level that fear is beginning to subvert reason.

The argument that a nuclear deterrence strategy, which until now has underpinned the arms race, has succeeded in keeping the peace between East and West for nearly 40 years cannot be

21

easily dismissed. But, as nuclear weapons proliferate and the destructive power of those weapons becomes more apocalyptic, the proposition that we must have this massive capacity to annihilate ourselves totally has lost all credibility.

The arms race pollutes the ethical stream of human survival not only by threatening man's physical existence but also by impairing his prospects for development, particularly the more balanced and sustainable development now widely recognized as essential. When almost one trillion dollars are devoted every year to military expenditure, when the great majority of the world's scientists, engineers and technicians are engaged in military-related research or production, when the military culture becomes paramount in the corridors and council chambers of world power and spreads even to the developing world, real development is not only neglected, it is negated. This is the case for all countries, rich and poor, but with the most devastating consequences for the poorest.

One of the most tragic consequences of a civilization geared for war rather than peace is the rapid spread of militarization throughout the countries of the Third World, in defiance of the evident gravity of developmental need. One quarter of the Third World's crippling debt burden of nearly $1,000 billion results from arms purchases. While Third World arms imports have fallen recently, due partly to declining oil revenue and to the debt crisis, Third World arms industries have continued to grow, with over fifty developing countries having their own arms industries by 1985.

The reality behind these facts is of a world in which the insecurity of its people is increasing, not diminishing; a world failing to work to create a climate of peace and international understanding conducive to meeting the great challenges of our time; a world squandering its treasure on the worthless dross of armaments and denying vast resources to the needs of human development. Armed violence, and the atmosphere of distrust which feeds it, call for our most urgent attention. The technical knowledge to bring about disarmament exists but the realization of world peace and global security require a new humanitarian commitment from all of us.

Terrorism

Failures within the international community to respond to aspirations of nationhood, and to resolve deep-seated communal and racial grievances have all too frequently led to acts of terrorism. Terrorism is by no means a new phenomenon. The term is used, sometimes wrongly, to describe a wide variety of violent activities, but is usually understood to mean the use or threat of violence designed to achieve a political purpose by individuals or small groups. As such, it has much in common with the actions of resistance movements in territories occupied by hostile forces, a comparison which immediately suggests the ambiguities inherent in the word terrorist, since one man's terrorist may be another's resistance or freedom-fighter.

Unlike earlier forms of it, modern terrorism often takes place far from the country or regime against which its acts are directed, and adds hostage-taking to the political assassinations of earlier times.

For terrorist action to have the required effect of striking terror or achieving a particular political aim, it must have as widespread an impact as possible. The contemporary global community offers an ideal echo-chamber. Modern media coverage together with the new information technology means that news of the action can reach a mass audience within minutes of its occurrence.

Terrorism has become in recent years a serious impediment to the development of international co-operation and multi-lateralism. It is part of a spectrum of global violence and reflects the increasing reliance on violent methods. These methods are not employed only by aggrieved groups but also by governments to harass opponents. According to the United Nations, 'disappearances', kidnapping, torture and murder are practised by governments, or by para-military groups protected by them, in almost forty countries. This particular form of terrorism received our special attention and is discussed later in this Report.

Terrorism is an affront to humanity. It violates the principles of international co-operation and understanding between nations which are central to an international humanitarian perspective. It can only be combated effectively through

23

collective action, tenaciously pursued at the global level on the basis of common principles.

The International Drug Problem

Illicit drug trafficking is one of the most lucrative forms of international trade with profits running into billions of dollars. In the United States, the retail value of the illicit drug trade, an estimated $125 billion, is bigger than most of the giant business corporations. In poor countries, drug money is capable of transforming national economies and undermining fragile political structures.

International crime syndicates are directly connected with the illicit drug trade and launder profits through established financial institutions. The full extent of such transactions is difficult to quantify in the absence of access to bank records but a significant proportion is reportedly recycled for investment in orthodox business ventures. Drug money also appears to be closely associated with the international arms trade and is an important element in several on-going armed conflicts.

Contrary to the general view of illicit drug use and narcotic flows which tends to see drug addiction as a problem faced mainly by industrialized countries as a result of opium poppy and coca cultivation in the Third World, facts and figures tell a different story. The bulk of opium production is used locally with a staggering 60 per cent of the world's heroin supply consumed in Asia. Up till now, activities aimed at cutting off supplies have been a major preoccupation of the authorities. This has led to the processing facilities being set up closer to the point of production, which, in turn, has resulted in higher consumption levels and social and economic disruption in Third World countries. Often crop eradication programmes in one area have led to increased production elsewhere.

Crop substitution programmes have had equally ambiguous results. In general, they have shown little appreciation of the social and cultural setting and economic imperatives which favour the cultivation of crops used in the illicit production of narcotics. While the income made by the peasant farmers is negligible as compared to the retail value of illicit drugs, for many it is their only means of survival.

Law enforcement measures aimed at thwarting supply routes and penalizing or regulating the distribution and consumption of intoxicants, are effective methods to curb drug abuse. Strengthened police activities are almost an automatic response when the prevalence of drug addiction increases or becomes an issue that commands public attention. However, one of the major pitfalls of a law-enforcement approach is the tendency to narrow the focus to cutting off supplies and the justification of measures, however inappropriate, aimed at realizing this objective. Some countries have resorted to draconian legislation, including the death penalty, for possession of a prohibited drug.

On a practical level, treating drug addicts as criminals does not resolve the problem. Those who direct and control the illicit drug trade are rarely prosecuted. Notwithstanding sophisticated surveillance technology, stronger patrols and bigger budgets, police and customs officials can, at best, hope to intercept between 3 and 10 per cent of drugs illicitly entering a country.

A more realistic assessment of the poverty and chronic underdevelopment which characterize the production of crops in source countries would greatly benefit the formulation of programmes geared to peasants' needs as opposed to the current emphasis on eradicating drug-producing crops. Crop-substitution programmes have an important role to play in combating drug abuse but must take into account the cultural, social and economic situation of the people most directly affected.

Drug abuse and trafficking have emerged as a threat not just to a few countries but to the world community as a whole. The repercussions tend to go beyond the problem of drugs to arms trafficking and national security. To date, however, our international system has been largely ineffective in reducing the impact of this trade on human lives. It seems more urgent than ever that the system of multilateral co-operation is strengthened to find a global response to this growing problem.

3.   Forces of Change

"Change is the law of life. And those who look only to the past or the present are certain to miss the future."

John F. Kennedy, 1963

The great issues of our time – and we have identified only some of the most pressing – affect us all and can only be confronted globally. But our future depends not merely on finding technical solutions to the problems we face, but also on reaching a consensus about the ethical basis for our response. We believe that while there is no ready-made, universally accepted humanitarian code, there are a number of common values and important actors on the world scene whose influence can be, albeit not necessarily, a powerful force for positive change.

In identifying some of the potent new forces on the world stage – the newly independent nations, peoples' organizations, women's movements, the young, new technology, transnational corporations and the media – we are aware of the omission of many other significant actors. We believe, however, that mention must be made of some of those who in our view can contribute significantly to the shaping of our future world. Our intention is not to discuss the role of these actors in detail, but to indicate how they play a part in posing humanitarian challenges and moulding humanitarian responses.

The New Nations

The most dynamic factor in the post-1945 world has been the emergence of more than one hundred new nations as a result of decolonization. The principal effect of this multiplication of States has been the inclusion on the agendas of international organizations of a range of issues arising from the human needs of the great mass of people in the Third World. Coalitions of prominent figures from both North and South have come together to promote Third World issues. Development forms the core of these issues: development seen not simply as 'aid', but rather as a collective human aspiration to a basic level of existence. Without food and shelter, rights such as freedom of expression and of political participation may well appear secondary. Without literacy, freedom of the press may lose its significance. Moreover, basic security without which development cannot take place, is constantly threatened by the arms race.

In addition to their actions at the international level, the new nations have formed a number of organizations to pursue their objectives. They have been successful in raising broad humanitarian issues relevant to the Third World, but their capacity to promote these issues successfully in the global context has remained limited.

Nationalism is a dynamic creative force in many parts of the world today, especially in the new countries of the Third World, but it is also a cause of conflict. Newly independent Third World States and other non-dominant States are naturally protective of what they conceive as their territorial integrity. Very often, East–West struggles intrude upon Third World conflicts where they are fought out by proxy. Some wars are underscored by racial or religious divisions. A substantial proportion of conflicts in the Third World result from the existence of borders created by the former colonizers which divide ethnic groups.

At the same time, the power of the nation State has greatly increased in relation to the individual. While the individual has also become more aware and able to control the material environment, many contemporary developments have tended to concentrate power increasingly in the hands of the State. This has frequently led to the abrogation of civil rights and even repression of political opponents, ethnic and religious minorities and indigenous peoples. As a result, an increasing number of peoples have been displaced, deprived or rendered homeless.

Nationalism, if it is to be a positive force, must include the protection of all human rights including political rights and the cultures and religions of ethnic or indigenous groups. This is one of the great challenges of our times, and one humankind generally must not shirk.

Peoples' Movements

There are a variety of causes animating peoples' movements: the threat of nuclear destruction; environmental issues; mass hunger in the Third World; apartheid; torture and illegal detention. Mobilization by people and communities is not new. But what is comparatively new is the extent to which contemporary movements transcend national boundaries.

Issues such as the arms race, famine and other man-made disasters have brought people from different nations and cultures closer together. In recent years, people more than governments have responded to the shameful spectres of hunger and starvation in a world of abundance. Indeed, left to governments, the global response to famine in Africa would not have been worthy of our common humanity. The storage of grain and butter mountains in the Western countries, for example, was costing billions of dollars while hundreds of thousands died of hunger and malnutrition in Africa. Yet despite the relative indifference of governments, people acted on their own recognition of the starving as their neighbours on an increasingly small and fragile planet. There are resonances of this spirit in the wider fields of development and environmental protection.

Another challenge identified by people worldwide is that of apartheid. The anti-apartheid cause is a human issue comparable to some of the great struggles over the ages against injustices such as serfdom, slavery and colonization. Left to governments alone, it might not be as seriously challenged. That it faces the opposition of nearly the entire world community is due to peoples' campaigns which have forced governments to take a stand. Ordinary people throughout the world recognize the moral and political imperative to end apartheid and demonstrate tangibly their solidarity with its victims.

Such popular campaigns inspire hope that many other major humanitarian issues will be addressed. Today, peoples' movements have become an essential factor to bring about change.

Women

Women have long been subject to political, economic, social and cultural discrimination in many widely differing societies. They generally have begun to achieve substantial measures of equality only in the last 100 years. In recognition of the need for international efforts to improve the lives and status of women, the United Nations designated the years 1975–85 as the UN Decade for Women. The United Nations estimated that women, although constituting half the world's population, perform nearly two-thirds of the world's labour yet receive only one-tenth of its income and own less than one-hundredth of its property. They have traditionally had much less access to education and vocational training.

The Decade derived great impetus from the growth of women's movements worldwide over the last 20 years. Its scope and impact was global. It was concerned with the issue of economic equality and independence for women, as well as their full integration into the decision-making processes in national society. It called for the restructuring of society and family life to enable women to participate fully in and benefit from development. The important role of women in agriculture in the Third World was recognized. The Decade had a major impact in raising awareness of the position of women and gaining government commitment to address their needs. Women, particularly in the Third World, are now recognized as the major food producers and processors, providers of water and energy, and providers of health care. Everywhere, they are beginning to work increasingly in the non-traditional sectors such as industry, trade, marketing and services.

Discrimination against women is incompatible with an international humanitarian ethic and contrary to fundamental norms of international human rights law. It is encouraging that the global women's movement has already had a substantial impact on the content and thrust of politics in many countries, not only by insisting on the inclusion of issues relating to their lives and status in political agendas, but also by affecting the way other issues are perceived, such as the issue of violence and exploitation to which many of them are subjected.

Women are among the leading new forces on the international

scene. The prospect of their full participation in society at all levels – local, national and international – is one of the greatest sources of hope for the establishment of a new humanitarian order in world affairs. However, in many traditional societies, that promise is still far from fulfilment. A humanitarian ethic would seek to initiate changes in societies which oppress and suppress women. It would also facilitate the rapid rise to equality for women. In a number of governments, special ministries or departments have been established to deal with issues related to women and to defend their rights. We hope that others will follow this path in order to increase public awareness of the issues involved and to reverse traditional practices and attitudes regarding women that are an affront to basic human values.

Youth

As well as peoples' movements and women's organizations, another group which deserves special consideration is the worldwide constituency of youth. A youth culture began to gain momentum following the Second World War in the industrialized world and has since spread all over the globe. Over time, this phenomenon has had profound effects reaching beyond young people themselves. In time, as their numbers continue to grow, the young will be the single most potent force to shape society. It is estimated that by the end of the next decade, those below 30 years of age will constitute almost 60 per cent of the world population.

In the richer countries, young people have considerable purchasing power which influences the direction of economic activities. In leisure pursuits, and particularly those involving television, radio, popular music, film-making and fashions, they are powerful shapers of popular taste. Their culture is becoming increasingly disseminated worldwide. Their views have a growing influence on those in power. They are to be reckoned with as a force that will mould the political, economic and social structures of the future.

Young people are at present often manipulated. Their interests are frequently exploited for commercial, political or other reasons. It is understandable and to be welcomed that young people are demanding greater participation in decision-making in areas of human activity which closely affect them. Moreover, young people in all societies, rich and poor, have been particular victims of widespread unemployment. It is important that education systems are geared to gainful employment and the job markets are adjusted to meet the new challenges they face.

Yet despite their serious special problems, young people, including many who are unemployed, are succeeding in acting as forces for change. There is evidence that young people feel particularly involved and committed to socio-economic development issues, to independence and to peace. They have demonstrated a particular enthusiasm and facility for fostering international understanding.

On the other hand, there is also evidence of increasing alienation of the young, particularly among those living in cities. Among the poor, there is anger and frustration and a growing tendency to use violence as a means to change their circumstances. Whether as soldiers or terrorists, freedom-fighters or rebels, delinquents or demonstrators, they pose a threatening challenge to political stability and social order in many parts of the world. Their natural zeal and energy need to be channelled, through imaginative projects supported by governments and communities, to constructive purposes. Constituting the majority of the world's populations, their needs and aspirations must receive the highest priority on the agendas of governments and the world community at large. Timely action is called for to avoid extremism among the young.

Modern Technology

Since the 1970s, many people have increasingly come to fear that technological innovation matters more than preserving cultural identity or social traditions; that it will be the values of efficiency, reliability, speed and predictability that will prevail in future societies; that we must adjust to each new invention or drown in the indignity of not being modern. Much of the debate

31

about development is turning to talk of technological revolutions capable of so radically changing the quality and characteristics of human existence that the past seems no more than a prologue to the awe-inspiring future that awaits us. Technology all too often seems enveloped in its own mystique – complex, remote, obliging us to bow down in fear and fascination.

The present concentration of highly active scientific research and of major technological achievements in a few countries should not obscure the fact that many cultures and societies have contributed to modern science, as can be seen by the study of, for instance, Chinese, Indian or Islamic sciences. Nor should prosperity be attributed to scientific achievements alone: colonization of new lands and the exploitation of their wealth contributed to the economic growth of a few countries and increased the gap between them and the rest of the world.

Modern science and technology derive their prestige from their contribution to economic growth in the industrialized countries. Only a few countries are in the forefront of advancing new technologies; others are essentially adapting to changes originating elsewhere. However, for large low-income countries, such as Brazil, China or India, there is a substantial capacity for indigenous development of a wide range of technologies. For small States, options may be more limited but are by no means closed. In fact, some of the smaller States are doing very well in relative terms.

Technological innovation has been vital to economic growth by raising the productivity of human, capital and natural resources. However, the relation between technology and growth is a very complex one. Technological advance does not necessarily imply scientific progress nor does it always mean economic growth. Technological inventions are tools which, according to the way they are used, widen or narrow our scope for action, and enhance or diminish our control over resources. The changes they are now bringing about give rise to strong and often conflicting emotions. There is apprehension that the new technologies will be economically and socially disruptive, but also hope that the power and speed of technological change in communications may bring nations closer and foster a positive multi-lateralism.

An optimistic view is that less industrialized countries will be able to benefit greatly from advanced science and technology and could reduce the economic gap between them and the richer countries while bypassing many historical technological stages. Reference is often made in this respect to four broad categories of new technologies: micro-electronics, bio-technology, new materials technology and new energy sources including nuclear energy. These technologies can be distinguished from other modern technologies by the extraordinary speed at which their application is proceeding and by their wide scope which transcends narrow sectoral boundaries.

A less optimistic view is that the benefits of modern technology may be available only to a few. Today's new technologies arise from systematic research programmes, largely funded by governments and major industrial companies. Advanced scientific research is no longer carried out by scientists working in isolation with a few assistants handling relatively cheap equipment and exchanging friendly letters with their peers. It has become expensive team work and its potential benefits are of such magnitude that secrecy is rigidly maintained.

The development of science and technology poses intrinsically humanitarian issues. On its outcome depends an increase or decrease in human suffering now and in the future. Human beings are endowed with potential creativity but can realize it only in certain cultural, social and economic contexts. Humanitarianism therefore aims not only at limiting the harmful effects of science and technology and re-directing the benefits of innovations to the most deprived in society, but also at removing the obstacles to creativity so as to multiply sources of innovations in all contexts, societies and cultures.

The potential of modern technological advances to contribute to meeting the basic needs of people throughout the world has yet to be fully explored. A humanitarian approach to science and technology demands greater priority for producers and services intended to meet the needs of the poor. These include improving water supply and sewage disposal techniques; lower cost construction, transportation and renewable energy, especially for rural households; drought and pest-resistant, high-yielding agricultural crops especially of food indigenous to developing countries; and finally greater emphasis on measures to eliminate debilitating diseases and improve access to health care. A humanitarian approach also requires that, to the extent possible, new technology is introduced after genuine and full consultation with those likely to be affected by it.

Transnationals in the Global Economy

A concern for the welfare of human-beings necessarily involves a concern for their material welfare. This concern lies at the root of the effort for development in the Third World. The fulfilment of the potential of every individual which is the ultimate goal of development cannot occur without a minimum level of material well-being. Below that level, both the rights and the powers of the individual are so restricted that effective choices to initiate personal development cannot be made.

Nothing illustrates better the global reach of current commercial methods than the activities of the transnational corporations. Transnationals, broadly defined, are the largest private commercial concerns on earth. The total value of foreign direct investment by transnationals in 1986 was over $700 billion, with annual flows totalling about $50 billion, only one-quarter of which went to developing countries. With the growing globalization of capital markets, there is vast potential for transnational investment. However, the social and humanitarian implications of the globalization of the economy have been by and large ignored while the financial power of transnationals continues to increase. It is estimated that the total capitalization of markets for bonds, equities, precious metals and mortgages is $11 trillion. Transnationals, particularly in their relationship to developing countries, pose special problems of a humanitarian nature.

Transnationals operate in a territory of their own definition both within and between nations. Though private, non-governmental and operated for the profit of individuals, they often possess the high degree of organization as well as the access to sophisticated technology and massive capital resources more typical of governments than of private individuals. They have established international networks of related companies, each of which may possess substantial economic power in the country – very often developing – where it is located. The fact that some transnational corporations have financial turnovers in excess of the public expenditure budgets and sometimes even the gross national products of quite a few smaller developing countries, gives them a power in some cases as great or greater than that of national governments. From a humanitarian viewpoint, this power gives transnationals a potential for either contributing to human welfare or causing human misery.

Developing countries have looked with suspicion on these giants because they are motivated primarily by private profit rather than the interest of national development or individual human welfare. Nonetheless transnationals are often a valuable source of capital, technology and management expertise which developing countries badly need.

Over the years, developing countries have gradually gained experience in dealing with transnationals. The call for an improved regime of foreign investment based on mutual interest has on the whole been heeded, although some difficulties remain and the hoped-for increase in private capital flows so necessary to developing countries has not occurred.

Transnationals have sometimes been the targets of well-founded criticism for their labour practices. They have also been accused of industrial pollution. The grim example of the catastrophe in Bhopal has alerted the world to the potential hazards of industrial disasters.

It is essential that transnationals should demonstrate a high degree of social responsibility, in accordance with their privileged situation as 'guest' concerns outside their own countries and operating across borders. In such situations, the formulation of codes of conduct agreed by all parties concerned has been shown to be advantageous. Such codes of conduct should be based upon the core values of an international humanitarian ethic. Furthermore, a multilateral code of conduct elaborated and monitored by the United Nations, which seeks to define standards to be observed by both transnationals and governments, would be a valuable advance in multilateral co-operation and in the acceptance of humanitarianism as one of the motivating forces.

The Media

The increasing influence of the media – the press, broadcasting and films – is a feature of our contemporary global society. It has grown dramatically with the introduction of new technologies for communication, and for the reproduction, transmission and dissemination of information. For historical reasons, however, the major news agencies which collect and transmit news across the globe are mainly Western owned. This phenomenon of Western dominance has been strengthened by the emergence of radio and television, with their requirements of substantial capital outlays in the form of production facilities, transmitters and technical expertise.

The arrival on the international scene after 1945 of the independent countries of the Third World, with different national perspectives and priorities, has led to calls in international organizations for a more balanced network of news flows, to reduce alien dominance. However, there are suspicions that this initiative may mask a desire by some Third World governments for increased control, censorship and manipulation of news and information. In most developing countries, radio is widely used and is the most effective medium of mass communication due to the relatively low cost of output and receivers. The spread of transistors throughout the Third World is an important phenomenon of our time. Many Third World governments, in common with the centrally planned countries, own or control a substantial part of their national press as well as radio and television systems.

The position of the media raises issues which are important for human well-being. One is the relationship between free means of expression, such as the media, and individual freedom. A free press contributes substantially both to the creation and maintenance of a free and democratic society.

However, in view of the influence of the media it is appropriate to raise questions about social responsibility. Criticisms are often made about such matters as selectivity, lack of balance, trivialization and sensationalism. For example, a responsible attitude towards women, who are so often the subject of media exploitation and stereotyping, is essential. The media have a further responsibility to avoid national stereotyping and nationalistic bias. In developing societies, which are often struggling to overcome massive human problems of poverty, unemployment and lack of adequate health care, the media have a special educational role. Equally, the Western media which have the most powerful global reach, have also the greatest responsibility to foster internationalism. The modern media can either increase our awareness of the total human situation, or help to perpetuate attitudes of racial and sexual stereotyping and outdated nationalisms, thereby increasing divisions and disputes within communities and impeding national development and advances towards internationalism. The rise of expectations, fuelled by the television of the North, is already contributing in the Third World to the growth of a very consumer-oriented middle class.

The media are sometimes open to charges of neglecting more abstract or complex issues which nevertheless bear directly on the everyday lives of people – for example, the debt crisis in the Third World with its consequences for the urban and rural poor. Here too, the media can make a humanitarian contribution by investigating and exposing structural defects in the global political, economic and social systems.

The communications satellites which are so instrumental in increasing the cohesion of our global electronic village, and hold such rich potential for the future, are also bringing into being a new era of television and a more vivid trans-border flow of information.

Television via satellite can spread knowledge of different cultures. But it can also put the cultures of smaller, poorer and weaker countries at risk. There is a need for the more vulnerable cultures to be protected in the face of the random importation via satellite of other cultures which may have a destructive impact. Direct broadcasting by satellite, by which the products of one country can be easily received by satellite dishes in other countries, emphasizes once again that the people of the world have the means to become even closer to each other on our ever-shrinking planet.

PART II
THE VICTIMS

4. Armed Violence

"The motto of war is: 'let the strong survive, let the weak die.' The motto of peace is: 'let the strong help the weak to survive'."

Franklin D. Roosevelt, 1936

Our Commission acknowledged at the outset that we live in an age of increasing violence. We, therefore, set ourselves the task of understanding better the armed conflicts which abound in so many places in the world and of looking into measures which would help alleviate the suffering caused by them.

We believe that a stable peace can only be achieved through greater tolerance and trust among peoples and nations. These goals must be our ultimate objective. But until that time international organizations, States and the people themselves can take action to mitigate some of the effects of armed conflicts.

Besides the horror of increasingly lethal weapons of mass destruction, we were struck in particular by three specific aspects:

* *Firstly*, we were alarmed at the rise of expenditure by States on armed forces and weapons. This rise in militarization is affecting nearly all countries in the world to the detriment of social and economic programmes. Most serious of all has been the proliferation of weapons of mass destruction which now threaten not only the antagonists in a future conflict, but their neighbours and possibly all of us.

* *Secondly*, we were concerned at the spread of communal conflicts in various regions. Such conflicts arise from religious, economic, political and cultural tensions between peoples; they are often difficult to defuse and cause thousands of deaths every year.

* *Thirdly*, we believe that we cannot take comfort from the fact

41

that a major world war has not occurred for more than 40 years. There have been dozens of serious and prolonged local wars causing millions of victims, among whom are an increasing number of civilians.

The process of militarization is global and unprecedented in history. A glance at the catalogues of the manufacturers of weapons shows that there are arms for all seasons, to any address and to suit any pocket. There is a hypermarket of destruction.

The armed forces receive the immediate benefits of scientific and technological developments which they often control. Military equipment is more and more powerful, sophisticated and precise.

The balance of terror may have enabled us to avoid a Third World War but it has largely contributed to an increase in arms production. The distinction between war and peace which was still evident up to the Second World War is increasingly blurred. Violence hovers always in the background, ready to erupt anytime or anywhere. In other words, security is purportedly maintained by States at the expense of individual security.

Arms sales have taken on such proportions that they have become a threat to the very security which they are supposed to preserve. Given their complexity as well as the extensive research and development possibilities, the maintenance of modern weapons is difficult: they become obsolete in a very short time. The possession of the most up-to-date military technology has become the most visible sign of the technological gap between the developed and the developing worlds. Moreover, the arms race has made developing countries much more dependent and the cost of arms has considerably increased Third World debt.

Nothing at all in the past can be compared to the contemporary build-up of destructive weapons. The danger is obvious and threatening. There are 93 countries and territories which, today, harbour foreign bases or other military installations. Twenty-five million men and women are part of the regular armed forces of the world's States and over 100 million people are employed in defence-related activities. The two superpowers today have armies six times larger than during the years prior to the Second World War.

Together, the countries of NATO and the Warsaw Pact are responsible for 80 per cent of arms expenditure, the most part being spent by the two superpowers. On the other hand, even though the Third World's share is small, the rate of increase in its military spending is ominous: it has more than doubled during the last decade. Globally, military spending now amounts to some two million dollars a minute.

While disarmament must remain the general long-term goal, it seems to us that urgent attention needs to be paid to scaling down mass destruction weapons. Recognizing that questions of security and armaments are beyond the scope of our work, we felt, nonetheless, that the threat of total annihilation of human civilization posed by weapons of mass destruction must be emphasized in our Report.

Weapons of Mass Destruction

"The terror of the atom age is not the violence of the new power but the speed of man's adjustment to it – the speed of his acceptance."

E. B. White, 1954

Addressing the particular ethical questions raised by weapons of mass destruction* is critical not just to resolving the overall armaments problem but, above all, to ensuring human survival and safeguarding human welfare and development. From a strictly humanitarian point of view, contemporary achievements in the fields of nuclear physics, microbiology and chemistry should be used exclusively for the benefit of humanity. Instead, colossal financial and human resources are being used up in an arms race that no one can win. Given the exponential increase in world military expenditure, the growing risks of nuclear proliferation, the spectre of nuclear terrorism and the

---

* See ICIHI Sectoral Report: *Modern Wars: The Humanitarian Challenge*. Zed Books, London/New Jersey, 1986. Other languages: French, Japanese, Russian and Spanish.

militarization of the oceans and outer space, the threat to humankind is real. It calls for urgent collective action, inspired by vision and leadership, capable of reversing the present suicidal trends.

The possibility of global annihilation incalculably affects the emotional well-being of us all, particularly the young who are growing up today in an atmosphere of unrelenting apprehension. Myopic government policies are failing to consider the humanitarian needs of the future and focusing more on stockpiling weapons and increasing their lethal potential, than on identifying common-sense measures that can progressively lead to disarmament.

Despite tenacious efforts to promote peace and a growing awareness of the dangers and senselessness of the arms race, the stockpiling of weapons of mass destruction has continued unabated. This is largely due to the inner dynamic of the process, sustained by the military–industrial complex. In addition to finding ingenious methods of conversion of profit-making military activities to peaceful purposes, a way forward would be to approach the dilemma from the humanitarian point of view which requires States collectively to place the vital interests of over 5 billion human-beings ahead of considerations of sovereign prerogatives and national security.

Lack of Mutual Understanding: Much of the impetus behind the nuclear arms race comes from the suspicion and fear that one's opponent will achieve a technological breakthrough that will upset the tenuous nature of the existing balance of power. This is reinforced by the dedication of research scientists to technological advancement with no real regard for the humanitarian cost, and by a military–industrial complex with a vested commercial interest in maintaining it. National defence spending on nuclear weapons has soared, yet because of enforced secrecy, only a handful of people know and agree to the huge sums used for their development and deployment. This unprecedented situation has evolved through a series of ad-hoc decisions taken on grounds of alleged national security but made without reference to any overall global view of international security. Currently, despite the on-going negotia-tions between the superpowers, there is a lack of consensus, even among allies, on how to reduce the risks posed by mass destruction weapons. And because we lack a coherent international understanding, they continue to multiply.

Uselessness of Nuclear Weapons: The development of a workable framework for the management of the nuclear dilemma must begin with the recognition that the use of nuclear weapons can serve no valid or constructive military purpose. A catastrophic counter-attack, the slaughter of millions of non-combatants, widespread radiation, and the possibility of a nuclear winter would outweigh any gain that could be achieved. It follows that nuclear weapons ought never to be used. The only value of nuclear weapons is, therefore, to deter an opponent from using them. Even though there are inherent problems with the theory of nuclear deterrence, it is a relatively sane strategy as compared to the actual use of nuclear weapons. But surely no deterrent strategy can justify nuclear stockpiles capable of releasing more energy in a matter of seconds than the total used in all wars throughout history, and of killing every human-being many times over. A realistic step forward would be to move towards minimal nuclear deterrence.

Ethical Implications of Nuclear Deterrence: The aim of deterrence is to convince the enemy that the possible costs of aggression far outweigh any possible gains, thus weakening the military option of a nuclear attack. At the same time, the very threat to use mass destruction weapons for any reason is contrary to ethics and recognized humanitarian norms. However, for some policy-makers and military strategists, moral reasoning is unrealistic, given the present world situation and the fact that the actions of States do not yield easily to absolutes. In ideal circumstances, policies geared to ensuring human survival and well-being would lead to a world free from mass destruction weapons. But this involves an elaborate system of common and comprehensive security – a challenging task from both military and political points of view.

It is argued by some in support of deterrence that there is a difference between threatening to do something and actually doing it. However, normally, if an action is immoral, then the intent to carry it out is also immoral. In order to work, deterrence must involve a credible threat. This means that in threatening to use nuclear weapons, at least some decision-makers must appear to have the intention of carrying out that threat. However, it may be that those who bear responsibility for the decision to authorize the use of nuclear weapons have no intention of ever actually taking that decision. They conduct themselves as if nuclear weapons will under certain circumstances be used. But in the privacy of their own thoughts they know that it will serve no reasonable purpose. Nuclear deterrence thus rests on a bluff. People differ on whether bluffing is morally wrong or a moral necessity.

The most frightening aspect of nuclear deterrence is that it involves taking the risk of assuming that a nuclear power will be rational and exercise sound judgment. This is based on the recognition that the initial resort to nuclear arms will result in counter-measures too damaging to justify their use. The problem is that human-beings cannot be expected to be consistently rational. And in crisis situations, the level of rationality and sound judgment inevitably declines.

Some countries maintain that the fact there has been no world war since the use of the first atomic bombs against Japan is due largely to the existence of nuclear deterrence. The theory of nuclear deterrence may have helped prevent the use of nuclear weapons, but the past failure of other deterrents to keep peace for any extended length of time cannot be ignored. Moreover, it cannot be denied that continued reliance on nuclear deterrence, as presently perceived, presents awesome dangers to humankind's survival.

Horizontal Proliferation: Today, many countries possess the potential of joining the nuclear club. At the same time, the existing nuclear powers have done little to limit their stockpiles, thus contravening the spirit of the Nuclear Non-Proliferation Treaty (NPT). The slowness of arms control negotiations and the absence of convincing tangible results weakens the moral authority that the nuclear weapon States have to curb the horizontal proliferation of nuclear weapons.

Accidental Nuclear War: The proliferation of nuclear weapons hangs over our heads like the sword of Damocles. But unlike the sword, the radiation from this weapon threatens not just ourselves but future generations as well. Nuclear proliferation would increase the likelihood of inadvertent nuclear war. It is now known that human error and technological accidents have been responsible for numerous false alarms which could have triggered an exchange of nuclear weapons. The time between a nuclear attack and a possible retaliation is now so reduced that a due process of rational decision-making is becoming increasingly difficult to envisage.

In human history, no weapon was ever invented which sooner or later was not used, either in defence or to gain victory. The fact that nuclear weapons have been used is, ironically, a source of hope, for we know the horror of their use. In any given historical period, the level of violence in armed conflicts has been directly dependent on the weapons available. The acquisition of nuclear weapons by new countries, which may not have or may fail to develop the same control mechanisms as those countries that have lived with nuclear weapons in their arsenals for decades, is cause for concern. Moreover, the miniaturization of nuclear weapons has made them more tempting to use, as have technological advances in their accuracy and power, which encourage a pre-emptive strike mentality.

Despite these drawbacks, the weight of evidence suggests that nuclear weapons will continue to influence national policies for some time to come. Nuclear weapons cannot be disinvented. As long as the knowledge of how to make these weapons exists, they can be manufactured again. What can be done is to treat nuclear deterrence as an *intermediary stage* and establish minimum thresholds facilitating a gradual process of confidence-building. All of this can be tolerable if specific measures are taken to eliminate the perceived need for nuclear weapons and steadily bring about a change in attitudes at the global level in terms of what constitutes international security and the unacceptability of relying forever on the deterrent role of mass destruction weapons.

In September 1987, the United States and the Soviet Union agreed in principle to sign a treaty to reduce substantially intermediate and short-range missiles.* This is a promising beginning which we hope will be vigorously pursued and lead to more far-reaching results on the basis of identified points of convergence between the superpowers.

The Strategic Defence Initiative (SDI): It has hitherto been accepted that there can be no all-embracing defence against nuclear weapons. For that reason the Anti-Ballistic Missile (ABM) Treaty was signed and a measure of nuclear deterrence tolerated. A challenge to that position has now come with renewed interest in defensive systems against nuclear attack to be deployed in space.

The Strategic Defence Initiative (SDI), launched by the United States, has led the international community to be justifiably concerned with determining its status and implications for the future. An objective assessment of SDI requires that its attractions be weighed against the overall humanitarian consequences of its deployment.

SDI has been presented as a strategy for a more humane world. The possibility of rendering nuclear weapons impotent and obsolete is, of course, attractive. Unlike nuclear deterrence which is based on the threat of mutually assured destruction, a defence system based on 'mutually assured survival' is, in theory, difficult to criticize.

Effective SDI technology is seen by some as an insurance policy against compliance with any nuclear arms reductions ultimately agreed to among the superpowers. Colossal funding has been allocated for SDI and research is expected to yield new technologies in a myriad of civilian fields, including energy production, medicine, transportation and communications. History is replete with similar instances of fortuitous innovations. It is asserted that technological spinoffs which promise great gains for humanity are dependent upon heavy government

---

* Since the writing of this Report, further developments have included the signing of the Intermediate Nuclear Forces (INF) Treaty on 8 December 1987 between the USA and the USSR. It provides for the destruction of medium and short range nuclear missiles within 3 years and it permits on-site inspections. This is a modest but important beginning of a process which hopefully will lead to bolder measures in the field of disarmament.

funding for SDI.

No sane person can be against progress towards a safer and better world. The key issue is whether the chances of freeing the world from nuclear terror, as envisioned by SDI, are realistic enough to warrant the financial and political sacrifices that its deployment would entail.

The primary function of SDI technology is to intercept attacking missiles. This would require scientific breakthroughs in sensor and tracking devices to locate and follow thousands of missiles; computer programmes of unprecedented complexity to direct a response in a matter of seconds to a nuclear attack; and unborn generations of weapons that could transfer large amounts of energy almost instantaneously over great distances against small, rapidly moving targets. At any rate, SDI is based upon the assumption that detection, political decision-making, targeting and effective destruction would take place in a single minute time frame. Even if research could yield such technological developments, it is very unlikely that SDI can provide a foolproof impermeable shield. Even if one were to allow for only a 0.1 per cent error, it would mean in the case of a massive nuclear attack, the equivalent of several dozens of nuclear warheads. Undetected flaws in new, sophisticated technology are also inevitable. Moreover, deployment of SDI may not prove economically feasible. Projected costs run upwards of $700 billion – for a strategic system that cannot be tested under conditions that realistically simulate a full-scale nuclear attack. Consequently, the vulnerability of the general populace to a nuclear attack would always remain in question and a government could never have enough confidence in SDI to abandon its offensive nuclear arsenal.

Another complication is that SDI would be met with a variety of counter-measures. An obvious one would be to increase the number of nuclear warheads and aim them at major urban areas instead of missile silos to restore the threat of unacceptable retaliation. Saturation attacks employing thousands of warheads and decoys would make the interception of missiles during their midflight or terminal phase extremely difficult if not unmanageable. Reducing the duration of the boost phase of a missile and other evasive measures taken during the launch would pose further problems to SDI technology. An attack could also be directed against the vulnerable ground and space-based components of SDI to render its protective shield ineffective.

Even if SDI could intercept all land-based ballistic missiles, there is no viable way of defending civilian targets on a continent-wide basis against the broad variety of attacks that could be improvised to circumvent SDI. For example, as conceived at present, SDI does not guarantee protection against the use of bomber aircraft, cruise missiles, submarine-launched ballistic missiles, a smuggled suitcase bomb or indeed against small low-flying aircraft.

In psychological terms, even a partially successful defence of the kind envisioned by SDI could give rise to the temptation of launching a disarming, pre-emptive strike without sufficient fear of retaliation. Consequently, its deployment could be perceived as an attempt to gain a first-strike capability. This could undermine the stability afforded by nuclear deterrence and give new momentum to the existing overwhelmingly expensive arms race. Since the inception of the nuclear arms race, the development of new weapons has always been met with a successful response. For example, anti-aircraft installations were deployed to defend against bombers; intercontinental ballistic missiles (ICBMs) were developed to penetrate this new defence; anti-ballistic missiles were developed to destroy ICBMs; and multiple independently targetable re-entry vehicles (MIRVs) were then deployed to overwhelm anti-ballistic missiles. Logically, the unrestrained pursuit of SDI is likely to provoke a costly response wasting exorbitant monetary and human resources which could be better used for development programmes and other more direct humanitarian imperatives.

In economic terms, SDI research is absorbing an exorbitant amount of vital resources which could be constructively used to protect and promote human welfare. Although SDI research is expected to yield technological spinoffs which can enhance human welfare, it is more likely that discoveries having a positive effect on our well-being could be produced more cheaply and efficiently if they were pursued directly rather than as an unintended consequence of a vast military spending programme.

In legal terms, the deployment of SDI jeopardizes the

viability of the Anti-Ballistic Missile (ABM) Treaty which prohibits the development, testing or deployment of sea-, air-, space- or mobile land-based ABM systems. It was signed after both sides came to recognize that attempts to develop and deploy a complete defence against nuclear weapons would jeopardize rather than enhance their security. This conclusion seems to be as valid today as it was 15 years ago.

Although certain aspects of SDI may be attractive to some policy-makers, technological, economic, political and legal difficulties abound to such an extent that its pursuit threatens rather than ensures the prospects for a more secure world. Owing to technological limits, the original vision of SDI as a perfect defence of the civilian population is already in dispute. Experts now talk of it as a defence to protect nuclear missiles, not the people. Recently, SDI has been called an insurance policy for the period once all US and Soviet offensive missiles have been dismantled. This new vision of SDI, while morally sound, distorts reality. If SDI serves only to aggravate global tensions, frustrate progress in arms control negotiations and generate an arms race in space, then its pursuit as a policy of insurance becomes illusory and dangerous.

Fallacy of a 'Limited' Nuclear War: A wiser way of working ourselves out of the dilemma posed by nuclear weapons, is to ensure that military strategies based on their use are gradually and systematically abandoned. It is widely acknowledged that there can be no winner in a nuclear war. At the same time, it is wrong and dangerous to assume that war can be contained following the initial use of nuclear weapons. Not all nuclear powers recognize the concept of a limited nuclear exchange, and some have made it known that any nuclear attack, however small, will be met with a massive nuclear response.

The very concept of a limited nuclear attack is misconceived. Tactical nuclear weapons which have been designed for limited use under battlefield conditions can cause uncontrollable radioactive fallout equivalent to that released by the bombs used against Hiroshima and Nagasaki. Even if such weapons were aimed only at military targets, the collateral damage to civilians would be intolerable. Attempts have been made to enhance the radiation levels of weapons in relation to their destructive effect with developments such as the neutron bomb. These developments dangerously blur the distinction between nuclear and conventional weapons. The predicted technical breakdown in communication which could follow the initial use of these battlefield nuclear weapons would blunt accurate judgments about the kind of attack the enemy has launched, and thus increase the probability of a massive response.

Reduction of Nuclear Arsenals: A series of confidence-building measures are necessary in order to free us from the instability of the present global situation. Large reductions should be made without delay in nuclear weapons. This can be done without jeopardizing national security. Existing nuclear arsenals already consist of some 50,000 warheads when as few as 100 weapons on each side, 0.4 per cent of the weapons available, could annihilate all human-beings. Thus a much lower level than the present inventory of nuclear warheads could deter an attack and ensure that any violation of arms control agreements would not imperil deterrence against nuclear attack.

If progress can be made towards a conventional balance, it will be easier to make great reductions in 'first-strike' weapons. They are not essential for nuclear deterrence and only encourage the thinking which could unleash a nuclear pre-emptive strike. In view of the tremendous devastation which could be inflicted in response to a first strike, it must become unthinkable for any responsible leader to authorize such action. Yet because some political leaders fear the devastation to their country from even a conventional pre-emptive first strike, they have not been able to rule out in all circumstances a nuclear response. The danger of a use of nuclear weapons lurks where there is a perception of insecurity – a feeling that national frontiers cannot be protected by conventional means.

Balancing Conventional Forces: This would facilitate the reduction of nuclear arsenals and could accelerate mutual reductions of conventional arms. This is of the utmost importance given that they too can be used as weapons of mass destruction. It could also pave the way for nuclear powers who have not made a formal commitment to the 'no first use of nuclear weapons' policy to do so. As a first step, nations which now rely on nuclear deterrence should plan on a 'no-early-use strategy' and start putting into place alternative arrangements to prevent any side from being overwhelmed by conventional forces, in the event a conflict arises. Through confidence-building measures (CBMs) and a combination of negotiated nuclear force reductions and balancing conventional defences, it should be possible eventually to take the next step of declaring a 'no first use' commitment and stopping all military planning based on the first use of nuclear weapons.

Tactical Nuclear Weapons: At the same time tactical or battlefield nuclear weapons should be abandoned in theory and in practice. The use of battlefield nuclear weapons risks an unlimited nuclear weapon exchange. If they are not immediately eliminated, at least these weapons should be moved to less provocative locations. This would increase stability by eliminating the need to decide whether or not to use tactical nuclear weapons in the first hours following an attack, thus doing away with the 'use or lose' scenario.

The ABM and SALT treaties should be reaffirmed. This is necessary so as not to jeopardize the progress that has already been made. A new momentum to ensure a comprehensive nuclear test ban must be generated. The complete cessation of tests would signal that nuclear weapon States were curbing vertical proliferation, thus putting a psychological lid on a visible manifestation of the nuclear arms race. This would encourage more States to accede to the nuclear Non-Proliferation Treaty and make it morally difficult for non-nuclear States to flout world opinion and conduct tests.

International Humanitarian Law: Although no explicit international law exists regarding the legality of mass destruction weapons, several humanitarian conventions support prohibiting their use. Different provisions of the St. Petersburg Declaration of 1868; The Hague Regulations on Land Warfare of 1899 and 1907; the Geneva Protocol of 1925; the Geneva Conventions of 1949; and the Additional Protocols of 1977 prohibit causing unnecessary and indiscriminate human suffering in war and protect non-combatants. Since the use of nuclear weapons always entails the release of poisonous radiation which is certain to afflict non-combatant civilians, it can be seen to violate these rules of humanitarian law. Moreover, since the use of nuclear weapons, however limited, would annihilate civilian populations, it would constitute a crime against humanity as confirmed and defined by the Nuremberg Principles of 1945 which forbid large-scale offences against human life.

Several United Nations resolutions adopted by a majority of the member states have condemned the use of nuclear weapons. Already in 1961, the UN General Assembly Resolution 1653 (XVI) provided that a State using nuclear weapons "is to be considered as violating the Charter of the UN, as acting contrary to the law of humanity, and as committing a crime against mankind and civilization." This Resolution has since been reaffirmed.

The evidence in the field of law gives sufficient grounds for the assumption that the use of nuclear weapons is illegal. Not all national leaders recognize the extension of international law to nuclear weapons, preferring to rely on declarations of 'no first use'. Certain nuclear powers which participated in drafting the 1977 Geneva Protocols stated that they did not interpret them as affecting the legality of nuclear weapons. The strictly legal aspect of nuclear weapons has therefore been formally avoided.

Need for a New Sense of Responsibility: Major advances in arms control negotiations will require sweeping changes in the attitudes of all concerned parties. Nuclear weapon States must begin by acknowledging the fact that their security is not strengthened by attempts to achieve nuclear superiority. Indeed their security is more likely to be threatened by such a policy.

There is a need for an international instrument dealing specifically with the illegality of using nuclear weapons. It would be unrealistic to expect, given the current state of world tensions, that a convention condemning the use of nuclear weapons would solve the nuclear dilemma. But it is possible to achieve a declaration concerning nuclear weapons and their proliferation. Formal declarations forbidding the early use of nuclear weapons and, above all, committing States to crisis-control mechanisms, which establish fixed procedures for defusing tensions and for warning other States when tensions are growing, would be important steps towards global safety.

The sense of international solidarity upon which global security depends may presently be weak, but it can be strengthened and built upon. A positive step would be to link acceptance of no early use by nuclear weapon States with more nations undertaking formal commitments to prevent the horizontal proliferation of nuclear weapons. Acceding to the Non-Proliferation Treaty; the creation of regional nuclear-weapon-free zones; independent declarations of policy against nuclear weapons would all contribute to bringing humanitarian considerations to the nuclear debate and could influence ongoing arms control negotiations. At the moment, there is not even any consistent pressure on the nuclear weapon States to conclude a no-first-use treaty, though a precedent for such an approach exists with the 1925 Geneva Protocol on Chemical Weapons. It should be an important humanitarian objective to generate such pressure.

The Tlatelolco Treaty prohibits the deployment of nuclear weapons in Latin America. The 1959 Antarctic Treaty prohibits the signatories from undertaking any military measures or nuclear explosions in Antarctica. Hopes for the establishment of nuclear-weapon-free zones in Africa, the Middle East, South Asia and the South Pacific are growing, not out of a crusading spirit, but because States have come to realize that the renunciation of nuclear weapons is in their self-interest as well as the interest of the region and the international community at large. By open declarations of this sort, even the smallest States can exercise a catalytic influence in building a consensus against nuclear weapons. Other efforts such as the Five Continent Initiative, taken by the leaders of six countries (Argentina, Greece, India, Mexico, Sweden and Tanzania) and their thinking as reflected in the 1985 New Delhi Declaration and subsequent statements, raise the consciousness of the international community about the risks posed by nuclear weapons and signal the unwillingness of vulnerable nations to remain passive in the face of the nuclear threat. There is a great deal that the general public can do to pressure governments to act responsibly. In the past few years, millions of people have awakened to the dangers of nuclear war and become involved in disarmament activities, building a network of support across national boundaries. There are many obstacles in the path to peace, but they can be overcome if we join together in defence of our right to survival.

For a Balanced and Controlled Disarmament: In order to succeed, progress towards nuclear disarmament will have to be balanced and controlled. There is an elusive balance between maintaining sufficient retaliatory forces without threatening an opponent's security. It can, however, be achieved. The point is to move away from reliance on nuclear weapons without actually increasing the likelihood they will be used. Steps towards nuclear disarmament carry certain risks, but the failure to accept mutual restraints is likely to carry much greater risks.

Non-Nuclear Weapons of Mass Destruction: In the wake of attempts at nuclear disarmament, the international community must come to grips with another threat of mass destruction: biological and chemical weapons. With today's sophisticated delivery systems, the destructive capacity of biological and chemical agents of warfare is comparable to that of nuclear weapons. Because these non-nuclear weapons of mass destruction are inexpensive and relatively easy to produce in large quantities, they represent a lethal but tempting option for all nations, large or small, to supplement their arsenals and threaten their adversaries.

The 1972 Biological Weapons (BW) Convention: This is a far-reaching disarmament treaty drafted to exclude completely the possibility of biological agents in warfare. Over 100 nations, including all those belonging to the North Atlantic Treaty Organization (NATO) and the Warsaw Pact, have ratified this Convention which together with the Geneva Protocol of 1925 prohibits the development, production, stockpiling, possession and use of biological weapons. The Biological Weapons Convention does not, however, provide for mandatory on-site inspections to ensure compliance and only the Security Council of the United Nations (which is subject to a veto by a permanent member) has a clearly expressed right to initiate investigations into alleged breaches. At the time of the drafting of the Convention, experts discounted the serious military value of biological weapons because they were slow to take effect and hazardous to the user's troops, civilian population and environment. Thus the omission of rigorous verification procedures to ensure compliance with the BW Convention did not seem to be problematic.

In recent years, however, developments in the fields of microbiology and biotechnology have raised the military usefulness of biological weapons, thus giving rise to increasing temptations to subvert the Convention. Although it is not clear whether any nation has clandestinely violated the BW Convention, allegations have been made and a climate of mistrust has emerged which threatens to undermine the authority of the Convention. Since mutual confidence is indispensable for the successful operation of the BW Convention, there is a need to dispel any uncertainties about compliance.

All Parties must be willing to clarify any situation which may give rise to doubts about compliance with the Convention: to exchange data on research centres and laboratories established for handling biological materials that pose a high risk; to provide information on all outbreaks of infectious diseases that deviate from the normal pattern; and to respond promptly to a request for clarification of a suspicious situation. At the same time, there should be a distinction between official sponsorship of accusations and unofficial allegations which destroy confidence in the Convention.

It is imperative for Parties to adhere to these informal measures in good faith. If co-operation is not forthcoming, the viability of the BW Convention may be irreparably jeopardized. Up to now, the Convention has been instrumental in eliminating the threat of biological weapons. We must ensure that this humanitarian instrument remains effective.

Chemical Weapons: As opposed to legal machinery which excludes the possibility of biological warfare, there is no effective international instrument to deal with the dangers posed by equally lethal chemical weapons. The Geneva Protocol on chemical weapons of 1925 does prohibit resort to chemical methods of warfare, but more than 40 States Parties, including all the permanent members of the Security Council, formally reserved the right to retaliate with chemical weapons against any State which did not respect the Protocol. Thus, for these States, the Protocol is only a 'no-first-use' treaty which does not prohibit the development, production and possession of chemical weapons. States have therefore legally been able to produce and stockpile enough chemical weapons to threaten the life of every human-being on earth.

Despite a renewed interest by governments in chemical weapons, no one doubts that the indiscriminate killing of civilians and the human misery which would follow their use is clearly antithetic to the core of humanitarian principles. Studies on the military use of nerve gas in Europe suggest that the ratio of non-combatant to combatant casualties could reach as high as 20 to 1. Chemical warfare is generally regarded as underhanded and contrary to a war-fighting ethos. Yet historically, the outcast status of new weapons is often short-lived. After all, flame weapons, gunpowder and even the crossbow experienced considerable periods of military disfavour and moral disapproval before becoming assimilated into military strategies. There is an analogous danger that existing law against resort to chemical warfare will yield to military imperatives as stocks of chemical weapons multiply. This is why it is incumbent on the international community to take timely and effective measures, such as strengthening the Geneva Gas Protocol and elaborating a new comprehensive Convention.

Negotiations on a chemcial disarmament convention began in 1968. However, the requisite political will has been lacking and progress towards its conclusion has been disappointingly slow. Agreement has been reached on most of the substantive areas of the proposed convention. Each State Party would undertake not to develop, produce, otherwise acquire, stockpile or retain chemical weapons, or transfer, directly or indirectly, chemical weapons to anyone. The problem is how to ensure compliance with these obligations.

Verification: Unilateral, unchecked declarations of compliance by governments will not suffice to provide the requisite confidence to conclude a chemical disarmament convention. Unlike land-based missiles which can be monitored from the skies, military chemical capabilities can easily be disguised behind civil industrial development. States have recognized the need for rigorous monitoring procedures and all prospective parties seem amenable to permanent on-site inspections to ensure that all stocks of chemical weapons are destroyed over a ten-year period. But no agreement has been reached on how to ensure compliance after chemical weapons stocks have been destroyed.

For the most part, States are not opposed to routine on-site inspections to ensure against the new production of chemical weapons. Scheduled inspections are not inherently threatening to governments and provide ample time for them to protect their chemical industry against a breach of industrial secrets. It is possible, however, that the actions of one State may give rise to concern on the part of others which cannot be resolved by routine inspections. In those circumstances, a right to demand a mandatory inspection within 48 hours has been called for to clarify and resolve matters which have caused doubts about treaty compliance. It is this pursuit of the 'on-challenge' verification procedure which collides with the notion of sovereignty that remains the last impediment to a conclusion of the convention. There is now a great need for a compromise which accommodates both a nation's sovereign prerogatives and security interests.

A compromise proposal, submitted by the United Kingdom, provides for inspection on-challenge to resolve particular doubts concerning a State's compliance with the Convention. This would be a procedure of last resort, required only in special cases and applied independently of routine inspection procedures. But because a State receiving a formal challenge may have legitimate security interests at stake, there would be a very limited right to refuse an inspection in some highly exceptional circumstances. In such cases, the State being challenged would have the right to propose alternative measures which would provide sufficient information to clarify the matter. If these measures proved to be ineffective, further alternative measures would be needed until there was sufficient information to resolve the situation.

The proposal sufficiently protects state sovereignty and goes a long way towards reducing the possibility of a clandestine breach of the convention to a level which should be acceptable to all governments. It is encouraging that the Soviet Union has expressed its willingness to accept this proposal as a basis for a compromise solution once the contemplated procedures are more clearly defined. If all States can now muster the political will to eliminate the threat posed by chemical weapons, then international acceptance of a compromise proposal along these lines – for the safety of humankind – should prove possible.

In conclusion, we are of the view that even the most complex problems can be resolved through recourse to those basic human impulses which, although they are sometimes looked down upon by policy-makers, have helped humanity survive and thrive: mutual trust and faith in our common future. The confidence-building resources necessary to promote an international climate favouring disarmament are to be found within ourselves. What we feel is needed, above all, is a sense of urgency and responsibility – for individuals, governments and world leaders never to accept the status quo as being anything other than a dire threat to the survival of the human race. To re-establish global security on a humanitarian foundation, cemented by solidarity and a sense of common danger to humankind will require tenacity and an unshakeable sense of purpose. We believe that change is possible, if the pursuit of eliminating all weapons of mass destruction is accorded the highest international priority.

Communal Conflicts

Communal conflicts, ranging from sullen resentment and sporadic riots to protracted violence and civil war, invariably reflect the troubled society in which they occur. The incidence of such conflicts is on the increase and their scale has risen to new levels of brutality where reason and humanitarian principles have fallen victim to aggression and revenge. Communal strife is responsible for hundreds of thousands of senseless deaths and for creating even greater numbers of orphans and homeless people. The destruction of property and disruption of the economy which ensues undermines prospects for progressive development, leaving millions with a feeling of helplessness. Few countries are free from tension rooted in conflicting community interests, yet this subject has, by and large, remained undocumented and undebated at the international level.

Although there are some common denominators, communal conflicts are frequently complex and arise from a range of specific causes which rule out general strategies for prevention. Inherent in every communal conflict are diverse combinations of social, economic, political, cultural, religious, linguistic and historical factors which are conducive to fostering deep-seated antagonisms. While cause–effect relationships are, on occasion, easily identifiable, the factors which provoke and perpetuate communal conflict are more often than not an interwoven mesh of real and perceived grievances and threats to a community's status and identity. When specific grievances are not addressed because the means of doing so are limited or non-existent, tension mounts as frustration boils over to blur other issues.

Inequality is often cited as the key issue giving rise to communal conflict. Uneven development or relative deprivation in the form of structural discrimination in income and employment opportunities and limited access to health, housing and educational facilities which denies a group full acceptance into the larger society tend to intensify and politicize communal differences. Alienated and unable to redress their disadvantaged position through existing political structures, marginalized communities then turn to violence to vent their frustration. This in turn triggers a cycle of violent reprisals, leaving little room for dialogue and reconciliation. This phenomenon can occur in both poor and affluent societies, as shown by riots in such diverse settings as India and South Africa, Sri Lanka and the United Kingdom. In certain countries, population pressures on state resources may in the future stretch the resilience of political systems beyond their capacity to absorb more people and make the escalation of communal tensions almost inevitable.

While conventional wisdom holds that communal conflict is the product of economic inequalities, subjective conditions pertaining to prejudices, jealousies, prejudgments, stereotypes and other skewed attitudes also play a dominant role in producing strongly felt and emotionally charged antagonisms.

Recent years have seen the re-emergence of ethnicity as a strong social and political force which cannot be explained merely in terms of economic or relative deprivation. Members of a group bound together by cultural ties, history, language or ethnic origin often have their sense of group identity reinforced when confronted with any threat, real or perceived, to their communal autonomy. Without structures and mechanisms to deal with such threats, the situation becomes ripe for unabated violence.

Inter-communal hostility does not always lead to violence but there is an inherent risk of its doing so. Some States are based on fragile foundations incorporating divergent communities within artificial boundaries drawn by the former colonial powers. Lacking a real basis for cohesion or national unity, oppressed or disaffected groups often feel they have more in common with their ethnic or linguistic cousins across the border than they do with authorities in their own country. Increasingly, adversarial communities are aided and abetted by outside powers intent on aggravating internal disputes to their own advantage. This type of involvement can be an insurmountable obstacle to efforts to defuse communal tensions.

The State, theoretically created to safeguard the welfare of its communities, sometimes aggravates communal conflict by siding with one group against another or by pursuing policies detrimental to particular communities. Sometimes, state measures used to restore order after volatile situations have erupted are themselves instigators of further violence. Rather than easing tension and generating harmonious relations, repressive measures which deny fundamental human rights only serve to harden attitudes and perpetuate an ethos of fear and hostility which is passed on to new generations. Moreover, state funding for strengthening internal security forces often comes at the expense of economic and social developments which are essential prerequisites in bringing about peaceful change.

Given the respect accorded to state sovereignty with regard to jurisdiction over internal affairs, and the lack of adequate international machinery to mediate or defuse potentially explosive situations, countless victims of communal conflict have no effective means of recourse or access to external humanitarian assistance. Organizations such as the International Committee of the Red Cross are well equipped to help victims but are unable to do so unless invited by the national authorities. For the most part, existing international institutions are well-placed to render assistance only when a conflict spills over into neighbouring countries, or produces refugees. Too often, the victims of communal conflict are dependent for humanitarian assistance on the government authorities which may be responsible for their adversity in the first place.

The international community cannot afford, for ethical or pragmatic reasons, to stand aside and watch volatile situations degenerate into uncontrolled communal violence. In addition to leaving human misery in its wake, which offends our notion of common humanity and solidarity, communal violence is a malignant destabilizing force undermining the social fabric. Every effort, therefore, must be made to ensure that humanitarian considerations prevail to defuse community tensions, mitigate the human consequences of uncontrolled violence and restore order in the bitter aftermath of communal clashes.

Humanitarian Strategies: The antagonisms which lead to communal conflict are not insurmountable impediments in the search for peaceful and equitable solutions. Different communities have found ways to defuse tension – even after periods of protracted conflict – and live together in a manner which allows them to interact and settle disagreements before they disrupt inter-communal harmony and degenerate into open violence. Many States have developed procedures which allow disaffected groups or individuals a legal means of recourse if their rights are threatened or infringed. Both legislative measures which protect communities against discrimination and affirmative action programmes to correct disadvantaged positions have also proved effective in easing communal tensions. In some cases, however, more elaborate strategies are needed to prevent outbreaks of communal strife.

Measures to forestall communal hostilities include removing linguistic barriers to facilitate access to education and employment opportunities as well as educating teachers who have no understanding of, or sympathy for, the customs and traditions of communities other than their own. Textbooks can be rewritten to rid them of defamatory communal content and to point out the value in diversity of different cultures. The media can be a decisive agent for communal harmony by reflecting all points of view and disseminating information on the aims, aspirations, cultures and needs of all communities. Sensationalism which can mould opinions and shape attitudes at variance with healthy inter-communal relations can be avoided.

Neutral, third-party mediation may also be necessary to help resolve the most obstinate communal conflicts. Mediation offers a chance for leaders of adversarial communities to accept concrete proposals tailored to specific needs after a meticulously integrated examination of the particular situation has been conducted. In States where the level of tension is such that local authorities are unable to carry out this task, the opportunity for mediation must be extended by the international community.

Some conflicts are beyond easy reconciliation. In such cases, there is a need to delineate and make explicit humanitarian principles to restrain avoidable suffering and loss of life and property. Although any violent recourse to problem-solving is morally repugnant, acceptance of a humanitarian code of conduct applicable to communal strife could serve to protect those posing no direct threat to a community's interests. For example, children should never be a target of communal violence. Other principles might call for placing schools, hospitals, places of worship and localities indispensable for communal survival into zones of special protection. It may be far from a satisfactory solution, but national and international pressure to persuade community leaders to accept the application of humanitarian principles to their conflict with others is bound to mitigate some of the senseless violence.

The countless victims of communal conflict, in particular widows and orphans, have a desperate need for humanitarian assistance to alleviate their misery and prevent the complete breakdown of their families. There is presently no effective mechanism, either national or international, to provide assistance to the victims of communal conflict. Primary responsibility, of course, rests with the local government which has an obligation to compensate those citizens it has failed to protect. But in some situations, the government does not have the capacity or credibility to deal with the victims effectively. In these cases, there is a need for neutral humanitarian organizations to administer relief or for existing organizations to add this specific issue to their mandates or activities.

Conflicts occur at all levels of society: within families, communities, and nations, as well as between them. However, they need not tear apart the fabric of our societies if an overarching humanitarian approach is used to introduce sanity into volatile situations. The incidence and brutal effects of communal violence can be contained if governments and people join hands in good faith to ensure that humanitarian principles prevail in such situations.

We are of the opinion that governments which fail to protect fully the innocent victims of communal riots, must assume the responsibility of looking after them and compensating them, to the extent possible, for their losses. For this purpose, it would be appropriate if *at the national level*, special schemes are developed by governments for humanitarian assistance to victims of riots, in particular widows and children. *As for non-governmental bodies*, it is important to establish a network of local voluntary agencies specialized in programmes of community welfare, to take care of the victims, particularly children, on a long-term basis. The more affluent non-governmental organizations from the developed countries have an important role to play in strengthening the local voluntary agencies to cope more adequately with the challenges they face. Where such local bodies do not exist, financial support and training should be provided from external humanitarian sources to establish them and help them through the initial period until they are self-sufficient. As a matter of principle, emergency and long-term assistance should be provided, wherever possible, through the local voluntary agencies. *At the international level*, it would be helpful if the United Nations, within the context of a strengthened and centralized humanitarian apparatus, would designate a department or an ombudsman to monitor communal riots and the damage they cause and to help governments and non-governmental agencies in a purely humanitarian and non-political manner to provide assistance to the victims of such riots.

Humanitarian Norms in Armed Conflicts*

Since World War II, twenty million people are estimated to have been killed in local and regional armed conflicts. There have been some 150 such conflicts since 1945 and, except for 26 days of total peace, there has been an armed conflict going on somewhere in the world thoughout this time. Worse still, the role of the armed forces is growing in an increasing number of countries. Although we have witnessed in recent years a certain erosion of authoritarianism, soldiers continue to play the role of policemen in a disturbingly high number of countries. It is estimated that some one billion people live in countries with regimes controlled by the armed forces. The number of military regimes has increased from 22 to 57 since 1960. Armed forces whose task originally was national defence against external threats, are increasingly involved in internal conflicts, playing the role of self-appointed guardians of 'law and order' within their national boundaries.

In addition to the demands made by strategies of national defence, arms dealers always have something to sell to rich and poor alike all over the world. The weak and inadequate legal and protective machinery has not kept up with the ever expanding destructive power. With the greater number of violations, protection needs have also increased, but the means to satisfy them remain modest.

'Armed peace', 'no war, no peace', 'cold war' and 'war of nerves' are all ill-defined notions combining aspects of war and peace. Violence is a constant threat. At times it is kept in check; at others it explodes, and can no longer be controlled. Since war does exist, what can be done, apart from preventive efforts, to try and limit its destructive effects? How can the suffering of the sick and wounded be mitigated? How can civilians and their property be protected? In short, is there a moderating element

---

* See ICIHI Sectoral Report: *Modern Wars: The Humanitarian Challenge*, op. cit.

which could 'humanize' war? These are the questions which lie behind the emergence and development of humanitarian law.

The evolution of strategies and methods used in modern armed conflicts gave rise to an attempt to update existing humanitarian law and in particular the Geneva Conventions of 1949. This process culminated in the two Additional Protocols of 1977 relating to protection in international and internal armed conflicts. But many unclear areas and gaps remained after the Protocols were adopted. States were unwilling to accept any provisions liable to undermine their sovereignty. Many tend to regard political and humanitarian concerns as irreconcilable.

The existing protective machinery is complex. Each type of conflict now has its own hierarchically distinct protection system. The level of protection is very high in international armed conflicts, lower in non-international armed conflicts under Protocol II, lower still under the 1949 Conventions and virtually non-existent in situations of internal disturbances and tensions. The International Committee of the Red Cross (ICRC) does, however, initiate actions of assistance whenever possible and appropriate.

One of the main problems in conceptual terms is that there is no clear dividing line between various types of contemporary armed conflict which can exist side by side or follow one another. Unclear distinctions artificially maintained for political reasons do not make for an easy implementation of humanitarian law. Despite the progress achieved in the 1977 Protocols, there is still much to be done to devise a global humanitarian strategy ensuring equality to all suffering victims and adequate protection against the effects of violence.

The Protection of Civilians and Its Limits: Most of the casualties in contemporary armed conflicts are civilians, affected by massive bombing raids and the use of indiscriminate means of combat. They are also the prime targets of terrorist acts. During the First World War, 5 per cent of casualties were civilians. Today the proportion has reached 75 per cent and even 90 per cent in cases such as Lebanon. Indeed, it now appears that during armed conflicts soldiers are less vulnerable than civilians.

The 1977 Protocols reinforced the protection of civilians in two ways: against the effects of hostilities and against excesses by the combatants. The Protocols represent a major attempt to integrate humanitarian norms and ensure worldwide protection.

By restating and updating a number of well established basic principles which have now become part of customary law, the 1977 Protocols remind belligerents that they do not have an unlimited right as far as the choice of the methods and means of harming the enemy is concerned. They should not resort to methods which cause unnecessary harm. They must at all times distinguish between civilians and combatants and between civilian and military targets. Reprisals, the taking of hostages, attacks against installations such as nuclear plants and all means of warfare liable to cause damage to the natural environment are prohibited.

The principles governing the conduct of hostilities also have to be taken into account before using certain weapons and even before developing, acquiring or using a new weapon. Therefore humanitarian norms take precedence over military technology not only in war, but also in peacetime. A whole set of existing or potential weapons and means of combat are implicitly covered: nuclear, bacteriological and chemical weapons, geophysical and electronic warfare, radioactive devices, microwaves, infra-sounds, laser weapons, etc. The use of long-range weapons leads to a computerized battlefield and the actual soldier plays an ever smaller part. This in turn may give rise to counter-measures such as electronic jamming which can only increase the indiscriminate character of the fighting.

These restrictions caused a number of powers to refuse to ratify Protocol I since they felt that the lawfulness of the use of certain weapons, in particular nuclear weapons, might be affected. The Protocol, however, does not specifically rule out the use of nuclear weapons and this could be regarded as a serious shortcoming in view of the ultimate threat they pose to humankind and the very existence of humanitarian law. Nonetheless, Protocol I incorporates the fundamental principles of humanitarian law and this raises important questions. Would the use of nuclear weapons prevent unnecessary harm and spare civilian populations? Would their use be consistent with the principles of humanity and the dictates of public conscience referred to in international conventions? The fact is that the nuclear problems remain the same as before 1977. All Protocol I can be said to have done is to reopen the debate. It is therefore somewhat contradictory to refuse to ratify the Protocol after previously ratifying the 1949 Geneva Conventions.

The 1977 Protocols improved the measures for the protection of particularly vulnerable groups such as refugees, stateless persons and children, an increasing number of whom are affected by all kinds of hostilities. In that respect, it is not admissible for children under the age of 15 to take a direct part in hostilities. This provision is particularly significant in the light of the alarming tendency to recruit children into the armed forces and send them to the front after they have been suitably indoctrinated.

One of the Protocols' achievements was to lay down minimum guarantees for those affected by all types of armed conflicts. The individual is protected not only against a foreign enemy, but also against his or her own government. This is a clear step in the direction of protecting the individual against the misuse of state powers. But that protection, however minimal, is subject to one major condition: the existence of an armed conflict. It does not apply in peacetime or in situations of internal disturbances and tensions.

The Lack of Protection during Internal Disturbances and Tensions: International humanitarian norms are sometimes perceived as an infringement on state sovereignty and as an interference in domestic affairs. That is why, despite the adoption of Protocol II in 1977, the protection afforded in situations of internal conflict remains very limited.

In spelling out the concept of non-international armed conflicts, Protocol II restricts its use to conflicts of a certain intensity. It does not therefore cover situations beneath that threshold, namely, situations of internal disturbances and tensions. The restriction is particularly significant since those situations are nowadays the most frequent and widespread.

An internal disturbance is a situation where, in the absence of an armed conflict, the State uses force repressively to maintain law and order. The term internal tensions refers to a situation where, without internal disturbances, the State resorts to force preventively for the same purpose. There is no armed conflict, but the situation is serious and prolonged enough to prompt States to use force.

In practice, it is not easy to distinguish between disturbances and tensions, or indeed between internal disturbances and non-international armed conflicts. When does the maintenance of law and order become an armed conflict and vice versa? Who is to decide when a situation is serious enough for international rules of protection to come into operation? When faced with such situations, authorities impose a state of emergency throughout the territory or in the areas affected by the conflict. Excesses are frequent as is known only too well: mass arrests are carried out, people are abducted or are summarily executed, special tribunals are set up, basic civil rights suspended, prisoners tortured, etc. Every day in many countries in the world, basic human rights are violated under a state of emergency. The maintenance of law and order seldom ensures compliance with humanitarian standards.

A state of emergency is lawful under national and international law. What is not lawful are the excesses and violations it gives rise to. Very often, a state of emergency is used mainly to get rid of opponents or so-called subversive elements and to deny or restrict governmental responsibility.

In the present state of humanitarian law, there are no firm legal grounds for the International Committee of the Red Cross (ICRC) to intervene in situations of internal disturbances and tensions which involve not two sovereign States at the international level but a State and its own subjects at the internal level. So far, the ICRC has exercised 'ad hoc protection' mainly on the basis of its Statutes. Legally speaking, this is an unsatisfactory solution since the State is under no obligation to accept ICRC intervention.

The human rights instruments applicable in situations of internal disturbances and tensions are not adequate. Not only do they provide less protection than in the case of armed violence, they may also be restricted by the imposition of a state of emergency. The lack of humanitarian protection often contributes to a spiral of violence and a decline of the rule of law.

The Weakness of Institutional Means in the Face of Increasing Violations: The major challenge faced by humanitarian law is the great number of violations of existing rules. Attacks against cities and civilian populations, the taking of hostages, the use of chemical weapons and the ill-treatment of prisoners of war, all illustrate the decline of the rule of law and the frequent non-observance of humanitarian norms.

Several factors account for this situation. In recent decades, armed conflicts have tended to last longer and become more radical. All kinds of extremist tendencies have emerged, animated by groups or communities who believe that they alone know what is right and who consequently are intolerant of other beliefs or views. Such radicalization often expresses itself in various forms of terrorism. In this context, it would be helpful, for example, to mobilize humanitarian principles on the basis of the concept of the greater good and, consequently, support those States that refuse to respond to blackmail (through such means as hostage-taking, hijacking or other means) on the ground that they will save the lives of more individuals in the longer term if they are ready to take risks in the shorter term. A further complication arises from the fact that most present-day conflicts are internal conflicts. The participants multiply and the power structures change at an ever-increasing pace. In the case of internal conflicts, for example, it is often difficult to determine who exactly is in command and who is responsible for applying or flaunting humanitarian principles.

The institutional and procedural framework to ensure compliance with humanitarian norms is largely dependent on the consent and political will of States. The protecting power system and investigation machinery have never worked satisfactorily. The effectiveness of the relevant provisions in the 1977 Protocols is dependent upon the good will of States. It is regrettable that the *International Fact-Finding Commission*, foreseen in the Geneva Conventions, has still not come into operation. So far only seven States have accepted its competence. In the end the ICRC alone assumes the role of assistance and certain control functions but it, too, has to contend with state objections based on sovereignty.

Many governments seem to take a rather relaxed view

regarding compliance with humanitarian norms, as if by ratifying the Conventions they had been freed from all other obligations. But the most perfect of conventions will have little practical impact if it cannot rely on effective government support. By mid-1987, 165 States had adhered to the Geneva Conventions and their implementing and control machinery. But as soon as they are directly or indirectly involved in an armed conflict, most States qualify, interpret or simply ignore the rules of humanity, evoking state interests and sovereign prerogatives. Political considerations prevail over humanitarian requirements and humanitarian concerns are used to further political aims.

A Realistic Humanitarian Strategy: Concern over non-observance of humanitarian norms does not mean that these norms do not exist but rather that they should enjoy greater authority. More than ever before, there is a need to reinforce and revitalize rules of humanity which are often blatantly disregarded. But it is clear that to have any effect, solutions must be realistic and take into account the international climate.

It is certainly not by adopting new sets of rules of humanitarian law that better compliance will be achieved. The rules exist already. Indeed, codification could even be said to have reached saturation point. What is lacking is simplicity, clarity and, above all, efficient and effective implementation. The challenge is to ensure the observance of the rules we already have.

There are, of course, deficiencies. Some may be regarded as technical: they concern, for instance, maritime war neutrality or the identification and marking of medical transport. Others which have already been mentioned are more serious, namely the failure to prohibit nuclear weapons and the lack of protection in situations of internal disturbances and tensions. But as a whole, humanitarian law is rather comprehensive and covers practically the whole field of armed conflicts.

A treaty prohibition of nuclear weapons is of course to be achieved not in the field of humanitarian law but in that of disarmament. Only negotiations between nuclear powers may yield substantial results. However, efforts in a less formal framework could have a bearing on disarmament negotiations.

It does not seem easy, in the present context, to apply humanitarian rules in situations of internal disturbance and tension by a formal limitation of state sovereignty. However, it may be possible to ensure better protection in such situations by restating a set of fundamental rules of humanity in a flexible and simple manner.

Taking into account the difficulties being faced in the field of international humanitarian law and practice, we are of the view that the following general measures would be helpful:

i) A Clear and Concise Restatement of the Fundamental Rules of Humanity: A set of minimum rules combining fundamental principles of humanitarian law and human rights should be compiled to serve as a kind of code of conduct which States and state officials or soldiers would have to observe at all times. It would cover the following basic concepts:

> *The right to life; dignity of the human person; no unlimited choice of the means used to maintain law and order; prohibition of acts of terrorism and of indiscriminate violence; prohibition of torture and degrading treatment; respect for the injured and protection of medical action; prohibition of forced or involuntary disappearances; fundamental judicial guarantees; special protection of children; dissemination and teaching of these fundamental rules.*

The complexity of humanitarian norms and the lack of immediate clarity is often a cause of violation. Highlighting the basic principles of humanitarian law and isolating them from the mass of procedural and implementing provisions would be very useful since it would make both the principles and potential violations clearly visible. It would also define more adequately the actual conduct to follow in situations of armed conflict.

The need for clarity could also be an encouragement to spell out, for instance in a declaration, the basic principles applicable not only in armed conflicts but in any related circumstances, including situations of internal disturbance and tension.

Such an effort at the international level would certainly not weaken, still less replace, existing law. The purpose is not to trade rules for principles, but rather to achieve and disseminate an overall but simple statement which would strengthen humanitarian consensus and remove conflict between political and humanitarian interests. It would be parallel and supplementary to the efforts made to encourage ratification and implementation of conventional norms.

ii) Ratification of the 1977 Protocols: These two Protocols have not been as successful as had been expected in terms of the number and speed of state ratifications. By May 1987, 67 States had become Parties to Protocol I, and 61 to Protocol II. Many Third World, neutral and Nordic European States have acceded to the Protocols but there have been few ratifications from other Western or Eastern European countries. Of the five permanent Members of the United Nations Security Council – all of them nuclear States – only the People's Republic of China has ratified both Protocols.

Such reluctance is unjustified. In fact, the Protocols do not, as a whole, constitute new law. They merely update humanitarian law, in particular the four 1949 Conventions to which practically all States have acceded.

Protocol I, relating to international armed conflicts, updates the means and methods of combat and provides better protection of civilian populations by prohibiting attacks against them. The shadow of a prohibition of nuclear weapons can of course be seen behind Protocol I, and this explains the reluctance of nuclear powers – with the exception of China – to ratify it.

Another reason for the reluctance of governments to ratify Protocol I is the fact that wars of national liberation are assimilated to international conflicts and that it prohibits reprisals. However, on the subject of reprisals, all this Protocol does is to draw the logical conclusions from the recognized principle of protection of the civilian population.

Protocol II has also given rise to a number of misgivings. Several newly independent States fear that it might affect their sovereignty, in particular the right to choose their response to possible internal difficulties. But here again, there is nothing new compared to the situation prevailing before 1977. The only significant change is the greater protection of the civilian population and of persons deprived of liberty as well as the protection of medical services and personnel. Besides, Protocol II only covers internal conflicts of a certain intensity, and therefore does not extend to situations of internal disturbance and tension.

The concern expressed by a number of Third World countries which might face internal difficulties is unjustified. The Protocol cannot be invoked for the purpose of affecting a State's sovereign right or the government's responsibility to maintain or re-establish law and order, or to defend national unity and territorial integrity by all legitimate means. Care was also taken not to grant any status or privileged treatment to captured combatants. There is therefore no reason for Third World States to evade ratification.

International and regional organizations should encourage ratification of the 1977 Additional Protocols and ensure wider dissemination of humanitarian norms, as has been done in the field of human rights. Evoking the reasons briefly mentioned above, our Commission sent a detailed memorandum in 1985 to more than 110 governments urging them to ratify the 1977 Additional Protocols, as well as a reminder in 1987 on the occasion of the 10th anniversary of the adoption of the Protocols. A number of official replies, many of them favourable, have been received since then.

iii) Better Observance of Humanitarian Norms: States have undertaken not only to observe humanitarian norms but also, more importantly, to ensure their implementation and, thus, in the face of serious breaches, to act individually or collectively. This kind of collective control could be effective if it were used more frequently. It is in the interest of States to combine political and humanitarian concerns. Far from being incompatible, they condition and complement one another.

As for the United Nations Organization, when armed conflicts cannot be avoided, it should also try to mitigate the suffering caused by them. Missions of 'good offices' by the Secretary-General or the setting up of commissions of inquiry could, for instance, help improve control of the implementation of humanitarian norms. Moreover, making the public aware of violations complements the strategy of humanitarian organiza-

75

tions, even though the latter have to avoid denunciations so as not to jeopardize their action in the field and lose access to the victims they seek to help.

iv) More Vigilance During States of Emergency: The United Nations and human rights organizations can also ensure supplementary protection on the basis of human rights Conventions, especially in situations of internal conflict where humanitarian law has not yet been much developed, as well as in situations of internal disturbances and tensions where it does not apply at all. The effectiveness of human rights protection follows an opposite pattern in that it is high in peacetime and gradually dwindles in situations of war or 'exceptional public danger'. It is precisely in situations where the protection of both humanitarian law and human rights is considerably reduced that extra vigilance is called for.

States where such situations do exist should therefore be 'put under observation'. International organizations should draw up a list, to be constantly updated, of all countries imposing a state of emergency, with as many details as possible. They should also make known excesses which a state of emergency may give rise to.

v) Improving Public Awareness: Public opinion has proved an effective instrument in promoting human rights. It is regrettable that violations of humanitarian law do not attract as much public interest as violations of human rights. In the field of humanitarian law, there are no reports of the kind published annually by certain human rights bodies. There are also far fewer bodies to publicize and denounce violations of humanitarian rules.

Present-day conflicts are won and lost partly through the media. The media therefore have a particular responsibility in informing the public and increasing its awareness. Unfortunately, sometimes relatively minor acts of violence attract more publicity than armed conflicts which claim tens of thousands of lives. Information should also be more thorough. While many atrocious pictures of dying victims are shown, not enough is said about root causes and often nothing at all about the suffering that could have been avoided or mitigated if humanitarian standards had been observed.

A greater effort should be made, in our view, to protect those who send back information from the battlefield, namely journalists engaged in dangerous professional missions. It is regrettable that, despite multiple efforts in recent years, they do not enjoy so far a sufficient guarantee protecting and facilitating their missions. We believe that, in addition to adequate international rules of conduct ensuring their protection, it might also be helpful to introduce a universally recognized symbol, like the Red Cross or Red Crescent armband, to render their work easier and safer.

5. Vulnerable Groups

"All humanity is one undivided and indivisible family, and each one of us is responsible for the misdeeds of all the others."

Mahatma Gandhi, 1939

Our violent world is claiming many new victims. At our earliest meetings, we recognized that there were many especially vulnerable people whose lives were at risk and whose well-being was threatened. Foremost among those groups were *the young*: those in the cities of the rich countries facing unemployment and dispiriting alienation and those in the poor countries struggling for daily survival.

Many of us in the Commission have first-hand experiences in our own countries of the great problem of *street children*. We see them in our capitals shining shoes or begging for a few coins. It is easy to turn aside but not easy to ignore them, such are their numbers on city streets. Their very presence is, of course, a condemnation of our global society and we should all try to understand why, despite all our wealth and our scientific mastery, we still have young children living in such conditions.

We were not only concerned with the situation of the young but also with the growing number of what we chose to call the uprooted. In the last decades we have watched with alarm the swelling body of *refugees and displaced people* fleeing in search of a better and more secure life. Hundreds of thousands of others have been victims of *mass expulsions* carried out for economic or political reasons or rendered *stateless* by circumstances beyond their control.

We believe that much more needs to be done to anticipate these large-scale population movements, to contain them if possible and to ensure, when they happen, that effective humanitarian assistance is speedily made available.

Two further groups of people drew the humanitarian

concern of our Commission. The first was *indigenous peoples* – those first inhabitants of colonized countries or regions. There are an estimated 200 million indigenous peoples and in some cases their economic and social systems and culture are perilously near to extinction. Our Commission, composed as it is of men and women from very different societies and cultures, is concerned about the threat to indigenous peoples because it is a denial of our rich human diversity.

Another group which also attracted our attention were *the disappeared*. These are the people – sometimes political opponents but often innocent by-standers – who are abducted by para-military forces and sometimes killed without leaving a trace. Such intimidation and extra-judicial killing is outlawed internationally, but in some countries has been used as a means of stemming all opposition. We were particularly concerned with the increasing use of this practice by States.

The Young

"We cannot always build the future for our children, but we can build our youth for the future."

Franklin D. Roosevelt, 1940

The Protection of Children

It is a great indictment of our age that the victims of man's inhumanity are often the most innocent. Children, it is claimed, are our future. But everywhere, in rich and poor countries alike, they are the victims of abuse, neglect, preventable disease, hunger and war. It is probably a minority of the world's young which enjoys the secure and happy childhood promised by the United Nations Declaration of the Rights of the Child. "Mankind owes the child the best it has to give", it proclaims; children shall be given the opportunities and facilities "enabling them to develop physically, mentally, morally, spiritually and socially in a healthy and normal manner and in conditions of freedom and dignity". Yet the man-made disasters of famine and war claim them as remorselessly as adults.

In assessing the humanitarian issues of our times, we identified the situations of the young as a cause of priority concern. The young are the most vulnerable because they are the most powerless group in society. They do not have a vote and, with the exception of relatively few privileged children, they possess no economic resources. Physically weaker, children can be and often are abused by adults. In the course of our discussions we singled out a number of special problems affecting children: their economic and sexual exploitation, the effects of civil and armed conflicts, and their abuse within the family and in institutions and prisons. We also noted that the question of infanticide was hardly addressed by international organizations or governments and that female babies were, in large numbers, victims of traditional biases and economic considerations. Similarly young girls because of forced marriages and certain traditional practices were especially vulnerable in some countries. We were also aware of the problems met by children without parents or guardians, refugee children and abandoned children, and of the impact of inter-country adoption whereby children are taken from poor countries and sold to families in rich countries. We also recognized with the spread of terrorism the particular vulnerability of children as victims of abduction for political or economic reasons. Finally, we noted with alarm the promotion, through the media and commerce, of a culture of violence affecting children, ranging from war toys to the use of violence by television and other mass media. These are all serious and important issues and our list of concerns is by no means exhaustive.

The ICIHI Working Group on Children chose four issues for special analysis and organized in 1984 an international symposium in Amman to discuss them. They were: the situation of street children, children as victims of armed conflicts, the inter-state displacement of children and the proposed Convention on the Rights of the Child which is presently being drafted by the United Nations. The findings and recommendations of the symposium were published for the benefit of governmental and non-governmental organizations working in the field of child welfare.* Considerable progress has since been made in increasing public awareness and in promoting these causes.

We identified over twenty specific issues which, in our opinion, remain neglected in the existing literature and programmes relating to the young. However, limited time and resources did not allow us to study them all adequately. Two of them – the Urban Young and Street Children – were analysed and became the subjects of ICIHI Sectoral Reports to which we refer later in this chapter. There are other issues, however, which we believe should be studied further by governmental and non-governmental organizations.

Infanticide is generally defined as the killing of newborn children by or with the consent of a parent. The term is also used to refer to the practice of killing newborn children in certain societies as a socio-religious institution. Among some peoples infanticide may be perceived as a means of ensuring the survival of the community as a whole. For example, a mother may opt for the growth and development of a first child by doing away with an unexpected second child, especially in a situation of poverty or severe food shortage. Babies resulting from unwanted pregnancies or born out of wedlock are also killed. In other societies the male baby is prized more highly than the female. As a consequence, female infanticide is practised, particularly where there are restrictions on the number of children due to demographic pressures. In industrialized societies the incidence of infanticide is generally associated with criminal behaviour or psycho-social disturbance. Although it is difficult to verify, it is reported that some 400 societies in different parts of the world are believed to have practised infanticide either occasionally or frequently. Research on infanticide is limited to anthropological studies of specific societies or to sporadic medical reports. We feel there is a need for a closer examination of the subject, the circumstances leading to it and the socio-cultural context in which it is practised, as well as ways and means by which it could be prevented.

----

* *Protection of Children: Amman Symposium*, ICIHI and Rädda Barnen, Geneva, 1985.

The *effects of proliferating armed conflicts on the young* troubled us greatly. War has always claimed the lives of the innocent. Contemporary armed conflicts, however, are increasingly affecting the civilian populations. As we noted when examining the question of humanitarian norms in war time, there have been some 20 million people killed in about 150 armed conflicts since 1945. The majority of them were women and children. Children are also prime casualties in the conflicts between governments and resistance groups which are now affecting a number of countries. Apart from death or damage to health, inter-state and internal wars can cause deep emotional trauma. Growing up in an atmosphere of violence, witnessing the death of a parent or relatives and friends, seeing the destruction of familiar surroundings or experiencing eviction from home are all events which can have a long-lasting effect on children and can result in psychological disorders. In certain extreme cases, children have been abducted from their parents, tortured or sexually abused.

Children are also enlisted on occasion into the armed forces and directly involved in armed conflict. In 25 countries young men can go to war before they reach the age to vote. In countries torn by internal conflicts, children are recruited into the government and opposition forces under the age of 15 years, despite the prohibition under international law. New initiatives are urgently needed to mitigate the effects of armed conflicts on children both in the form of a worldwide consensus about such protection and a strengthening of existing international conventions and protocols to discourage recruitment of children into the armed forces. The present sanctions against governments contravening international instruments in respect to children are limited. Children, it has been argued, should be declared 'zones of peace' by being afforded special protection in times of conflict. We believe that this notion of the neutrality and safety of children must be promoted internationally.

In the promotion of a less violent world, the mass media have an important role to play. There is a need for greater efforts to reduce the number of television programmes and cinema films glorifying violence and armed conflicts. Often they spawn a series of comics, videos and toys for young children. The Government of Sweden, recognizing the harm done by the proliferation of war toys, imposed a ban on their sale. Other governments should be encouraged to take similar actions.

We were also gravely concerned by the widespread use and exploitation of *child labour* throughout the world, in developing and developed countries alike. By most accounts it is on the increase due to the economic recession in the rich countries and the persistent poverty in the Third World. There are an estimated 100 to 150 million child workers under the age of 15 years. The life they are condemned to is a cause for our humanitarian concern.

On the whole, in the rich countries, the child labour that was a characteristic of the nineteenth century has been by and large eliminated as a result of compulsory education, improved standards of living and campaigning by humanitarian bodies, trades unions and other organizations. Nonetheless, many children in these countries are exploited through long hours, low pay and exposure to hazardous and unhealthy working conditions. But child workers are mostly found in developing countries. They work long hours on plantations exposed to dangerous chemicals or doubled up in sweatshops, carpet factories or mines. The kinds of jobs carried out by children are almost limitless. If they work in small subsistence plots they may receive no compensation beyond the recognition that their labour has helped the family to survive. In some countries children may inherit a debt from their parents and be bonded to a moneylender or landowner for life, working only for some food to eat. Even where children earn some money from their work, it is pitifully small. For such children there is no period of carefree childhood.

Among the most disturbing aspects of child labour is the growing demand for young people for sexual purposes. The increase of child exploitation appears to be linked to factors such as the development of tourism and the establishment of military bases. *Child prostitution* has become big business in a number of Asian and Latin American countries with agents travelling to the countryside for suitable children. Poor parents are deceived into believing that their children will be well looked after and given legal employment. Children once forced into prostitution feel too ashamed to tell the truth to their parents and too scared to denounce their employers.

The tragedy of child labour for the developing countries is that a large proportion of the young are being denied education and training and the opportunity to contribute as adults to future development. They are forced by circumstances into a cycle of poverty, illiteracy, and despair. Too many poor families depend upon the income, however small, brought in by their children. But poverty and the overwhelming problem it presents should not discourage us from action. Parents need to be educated about child labour and children's legal rights. They need to be warned about hazardous kinds of employment and ruthless employers. Child workers should be encouraged to attend school and learn skills and above all not give up hope of a better future. Already some successful projects exist in several countries to reduce the more exploitative forms of child labour and to generate sympathetic awareness among the authorities. We believe such initiatives need to be further explored and encouraged.

In their programmes for the young, the education services, particularly of poor countries, have not always been imaginative and practical. Curricula and special courses do not as yet take into account some of the realities of the day-to-day life of children. The very youngest of poor children are often forced into premature adulthood. Schools, however, are not preparing them for the hazardous world they must enter. The education services, both formal and informal, also have an important role to play in combating the spread of street children.

The cities of the Third World have swelled and often not been able to provide even the basic amenities for their expanded population. The social and economic deprivation, while sometimes touching off effective community action, has also caused unrest, the break-up of families and the abandonment of children. Urban poverty and deprivation has, thus, forced millions of children out onto the streets, a subject which received our special attention and to which we will revert later.

We were deeply concerned by the increasing evidence of the physical and psychological *abuse of children* in the home. The circumstances causing abuse by parents or guardians of children are still not fully understood, but certainly the stresses of urban life – unemployment, cramped living conditions, inadequate social services – can contribute to the breakdown of family relationships. Children living in continual terror of their own parents, as many do, have no one to turn to. This sense of isolation is never so great as when a child has been sexually abused by a parent or guardian. The effects of such abuse are carried into adult life. We welcome the initiatives being taken in some countries to provide a sympathetic and confidential counselling service to children subjected to such abuses.

Children can also face abuse in institutions run by the authorities, and particularly in prison. We are especially concerned about the practice in nearly all countries, both developed and developing, of incarcerating children with adults, since we believe they can be both abused and criminalized. The problem is becoming more acute with the expansion of the prison population in rich and poor countries alike. Often children who have committed minor crimes are imprisoned simply to keep them off the streets. Clearly this is counter-productive. It teaches children to fear the police and authorities and seek comfort in an adult world, a part of which may be made up of hardened criminals. We believe that the authorities should pursue policies of rehabilitation rather than punishment.

There is still no international instrument protecting children in a comprehensive way. The Declaration of the Rights of the Child which was adopted by the United Nations General Assembly in 1959 is not legally binding. The Commission on Human Rights set up a Working Group in 1979 to prepare a Draft Convention to complement the Declaration. The Convention would, of course, make signatory States responsible for implementation. However, the process of drafting has been slow and the proceedings have not benefited from the participation of many developing countries. Nonetheless the draft Convention represents a leap forward in comparison to the 1959 Declaration because it will, once approved by governments, provide a legally binding instrument for the protection of children and their rights. It is hoped that the process of elaboration and eventual adoption can be accelerated.

Special thought must be given to the implementation clauses to be contained in the Convention. The timidity and ineffectiveness of such clauses in other international legal instruments is a major cause of the considerable criticism levelled against them. Innovative means should be found with regard to reporting, monitoring and enforcement procedures. Equally, strategies should be worked out for encouraging States to ratify the instrument.

The protection of the most vulnerable children will require more than words on paper, although they can have an important symbolic effect. Some comfort can be drawn from the fact that in the last decade or so numerous non-governmental organizations have sprung up. Their day-to-day work with children can be a source of ideas, information and action: they can push or shame governments into action and create awareness among the general public. In the end, however, children can only take their rightful place in society if all adults are convinced that the key to the future of our planet is in the hands of the young and that they consequently deserve much more attention than is being accorded to them by contemporary society.

The Urban Young*

If the present trends are any indication, it is estimated that by the turn of the century, about half the world's population will be below 25 years of age. At the same time, it is expected that some 51 per cent of the six billion human-beings will be living in expanding cities. No group is more vulnerable to the series of complex social problems caused by rapid and uncontrolled urbanization than the young. Despite the fact that they constitute the majority among urban populations of most countries, particularly in the Third World, urban planners have neglected their needs and ignored their rights. Without full awareness and urgent action on the part of the authorities and local communities, the tragic situation of the urban children, especially those living in the ever-growing shanty towns, threatens to become exacerbated as their numbers continue to multiply.

While the city has long been seen as synonymous with civilization, as a place of learning, of art and of entertainment, it can also be a place of corruption and decadence where the

---

* ICIHI Sectoral Report to be published in 1988.

young are exploited and fall into a life of crime, prostitution and drug abuse. Without adequate social planning in urban areas conducted on their behalf, more children than ever before are growing up at risk to dangers beyond their control. What is needed to resolve their dilemma is a pragmatic strategy which addresses, from a humanitarian point of view, both the causes and consequences of the intolerable strains placed on the urban young.

The most serious problem faced by urban children is inadequate or non-existent access to health care. Because doctors prefer to live in urban areas rather than the countryside, and modern hospitals dominate the skylines of cities in both the rich and poor countries of the world, it is commonly believed that children in urban areas are healthier than their rural counterparts. Recent evidence, however, suggests that this is far from the case, especially in developing countries. Statistics which indicate that people living in cities enjoy better health than those living in rural areas are misleading because they do not distinguish between different socio-economic groups and fail to include most shanty town dwellers, squatters, street children and others not officially registered as urban residents. City hospitals can provide health care, but the majority of the urban poor cannot afford it for their children.

Urban children are besieged daily by a variety of environmental hazards which are partly responsible for their deteriorating health. Inadequate sanitation; blocked and overflowing drains; uncollected rubbish; poor water supply; crowded, decaying and collapsing buildings; congested traffic; pollution from industrial plants; and vermin all take their toll. Malnutrition is rampant in most urban centres of the Third World and frequently leads to debilitating diseases and death. Single parents in urban areas with young dependent children most often have neither the training nor the time to earn enough to meet the nutritional requirements of their families. Persuasive advertising tempting children and adults to purchase convenience foods lacking sufficient nutrients for growing youngsters is also a contributing factor to the incidence of poor nutrition. Urban planners, primarily concerned with the demands of dominant social groups, tend to overlook the health risks which urbanization poses for children, and fail to design remedial measures on their behalf.

The only way the urban poor in both developed and developing countries have survived is by putting as many members of the household as possible to work. This is especially the case when the head of the household is unemployed. Where unemployment and low incomes are widespread, child labour assumes an important dimension. Although working children worldwide are mostly to be found in the rural sector, the extent of urban child labour is frequently underestimated. The law in many countries allows children to help their parents in agriculture or pasturing, but it commonly prohibits child labour in urban areas. However, in competitive economies, particularly in depressed urban areas of developing countries, most children want and need to work for their personal security and family's survival.

One of the effects of inadequate legislation and social policy is to push children out of the regulated sectors of the economy into unregulated and unregistered establishments where conditions are usually worse. When children work illegally, exploitative working hours, unfair wages and deplorable conditions become the norm. Jobs seen as too dangerous for adults tend to be taken by vulnerable children. Since they are usually subject to non-contractual recruitment arrangements, child labourers can be laid off without difficulty and cannot claim compensation for work-related injuries. And because children in many countries are forbidden to organize and are not represented by any form of trade union, they have no channels to express their grievances, even less to assert their rights. Without effective legislation and an urban network to protect their interests, millions of urban children are exploited by employers who then escape responsibility for the inhumane hardships they cause.

Aside from the debilitating physical and emotional injuries it causes, exploitative child labour most often results in depriving children of an education. Schools are often far from the child's place of work and school hours generally clash with the working day. Because of severe economic constraints, a formal education for many children is viewed as a luxury for families which depend on the income of their children.

The curriculum offered by urban schools gives rise to false expectations and does little to prepare children for the challenge of life in the city. Large numbers of children leave schools unskilled, unemployable and with frustrated ambitions. The failure of schools is often attributed to a variety of causes, such as problems in the family, poor teaching, inadequate equipment and buildings and lack of funds. Rarely is blame placed on the inflexible and inadequate education system itself.

The multi-faceted dangers confronted by the urban young cannot long be ignored. Urban growth weighted heavily towards the young will translate into insurmountable problems not only for them but also for the social and political fabric of the country unless an integrated humanitarian strategy is promptly devised and implemented. Locked out of the power structures which determine their fate, these young people look to urban planners and the community for a wise and determined effort to defend their rights and promote their interests. Without thoughtful and far-reaching policies and action, many of the urban young are bound to sink into apathy and alienation or revolt and turn to violence.

It would be unduly optimistic to suggest that the problems facing the urban young can be resolved in the immediate future. The challenge posed by them is linked to all sectors and activities of urban society and calls for a holistic approach. But a public awareness of the scope and scale of the problem, is already a beginning.

We therefore feel that in order to contain the situation, it would be useful for governments:

* ⋆ To ensure within the government structure a rigorous process of urban planning which takes fully into account the challenge posed by shanty towns and slums and which is sensitive to the needs of the young.

* ⋆ To develop effective long-term policies to contain the movement of rural populations, particularly the young, to the cities and provide adequate incentives and possibilities of gainful employment within the countryside.

* ⋆ To establish specialized departments to work with urban

The Victims

children in resolving common problems they face. The units
should have staff specially trained to address the basic issues; be
readily available to hear the complaints of the urban young; and
be authorized to initiate action on their behalf and prevent their
exploitation.

* To establish channels of representation for the urban young to
protect and to promote their interests and to mediate in disputes,
including labour problems, between them and the local
community at large.

* To introduce legislation aimed at prohibiting child labour in
those occupations which pose a risk to health and well-being
and, above all, to take effective measures for its implementation.

* To encourage urban policy makers to give higher priority to
employment and income-generating activities for adults as a
strategy to reduce the incidence of exploitive child labour in the
cities. Greater access to credit for informal sector workers would
improve the income of many urban families and lessen the
economic compulsion on their children to work.

* To introduce compulsory elementary education into all urban
areas. Governments, with the participation of urban communities,
should restructure the schooling system to ensure that it provides
urban children with relevant education. The curriculum should
be flexible enough to accommodate the schedules of working
children, and the use of non-formal educational methods which
combine academic skills with vocational training and income-
generating work should be considered.

* To develop rigorous guidelines, and establish advisory boards,
that circumscribe the extent to which advertising on the mass
media manipulate the values of children.

We call upon welfare agencies and non-governmental organizations:

* To operate remedial programmes for the urban young with the
participation of community representatives and to offer welfare
services at the locations where they work or congregate.

* To incorporate into primary health care programmes for urban
children income-generating projects for women, in particular for
single-parent women, and to facilitate greater access to child
day-care facilities.

90

* To launch an education campaign for health care which encourages the active involvement of the family and the wider group of people responsible for the young whether at home, work or school. The campaign should aim specifically at helping the urban community recognize the health needs and susceptibilities of the young. Above all, it should emphasize preventive medicine.

* To establish, in close co-operation with community representatives, counselling centres for the urban young suffering abuse, neglect and conflict which drive them from their homes. There is a need to clarify in legislation the distinction between runaway or abandoned children and juvenile delinquents.

Street Children*

"In their little worlds in which children have their existence . . . there is nothing so finely perceived, and so finely felt, as injustice."

Charles Dickens, 1861

In the context of the colossal challenge posed by the urban young, we chose to focus especially on a particularly vulnerable group whose needs or even existence is commonly ignored: the street children, homeless urchins who, in increasing numbers, struggle to survive on their own in virtually all large urban areas. Concern for their cause, hitherto largely unacknowledged, is long overdue. They exist in both developing and developed countries although their problems and needs vary. Mostly aged between eight and eighteen, and overwhelmingly boys, they are condemned by the indifference of others to fend for themselves, drifting from childhood to adolescence, brutalized and increasingly alienated. Their emergence was never foreseen in any national plan. They are with us nonetheless in almost all big cities, in all continents. Latest estimates put their number at 30 million, and growing inexorably.

---

* See ICIHI Sectoral Report: *Street Children: A Growing Urban Tragedy*, Weidenfeld & Nicolson, London/Sydney, 1986. Also published in Arabic, French, Italian and Serbo-Croatian. Other language editions to appear later include Japanese, Portuguese, Spanish, Thai and Urdu.

The conditions in which they live are little known, but have much in common with those prevailing during the Industrial Revolution in 19th century Europe. For most street children, staying alive from day to day and hour to hour means work: a hard, unending grind for a pathetically meagre return. In various ways, they all do so by scrounging, foraging, and bartering, by contributing, as economists blandly put it, to the informal sector. They shine shoes, wash cars, carry shopping bags outside department stores, sing or play instruments in buses and subways, or simply sort through rubbish dumps for objects to sell. When life itself is at stake, competition is ruthless, and stealing or fighting are unexceptional activities. Having been written off by society, many street youngsters hold its standards in contempt. Their life offers them the spectacle of conventional existence without integration into its values: proximity without participation. It represents instead a counter-culture which replaces school and has a very different syllabus. For them, the street is both a brutal parent and a capricious teacher.

To survive in such an environment street children coalesce into gangs. This provides the protection and comradeship of a substitute family and an acceptable code of 'honour'. It also meets the need for a sense of identity.

Like violence, drugs are rarely far below the surface in many neighbourhoods and represent a murderous underworld of their own. Among street youngsters, their consumption, a temporary escape from an unbearable reality, is almost universal. In some countries, marijuana is treated as a parallel currency. As drug consumers, they are often forced into becoming pushers, for selling drugs is one of only three ways, with stealing and prostitution, of 'earning' enough to buy the daily dose. Living where they do, street youngsters are also prime candidates for sexual exploitation.

The causes of such a disturbing phenomenon – personal, social, economic, and political – are deep-rooted, and do not lend themselves to any ready recipe for curative or preventive policies. Against a background of misery, violence and cultural breakdown, the failures of urban development and unco-ordinated policies all exact their human toll.

The child is on the street, usually, because his family is in crisis. There is often only a single parent. In many households, unemployment or underemployment leads to depression, the loss of self-esteem, alcoholism, and overwhelming strain. Extreme poverty invariably robs parents of the hope, strength, and resources needed to keep their children cared for. Under the stress of physical, psychological and emotional overload, relationships deteriorate, and beyond a certain threshold, 'home' ceases to exist.

Paradoxically, for street children, school is often not an open door, but a further constraint. In many developing countries, schools seem to belong to a different world, remote from their everyday existence. When classes are large and competition is intense, the number of drop-outs is invariably high. Few educational authorities in the Third World can afford to give much further attention to those who fall at the first hurdle. The content of education itself is frequently unsuitable for easy absorption in the employment market.

Many street children in developing countries come from families uprooted from rural areas and attracted to the city by the prospect, or mirage, of a better life. Children are always the most vulnerable in such a change, and the first to suffer from being uprooted. In the rural community, the extended family is always there to support parents and childrearing is a collective task. As they grow older, extra hands are more of an asset than a liability. In the city, economic and social conditions are largely reversed. Maintaining a child becomes expensive. Extended families are left behind. The role of the elderly, previously so important, is reduced. Other, quite different, social causes can also produce the same final result: the offspring of prostitutes, illegitimate children disowned by a 'respectable' parent, the children of political detainees, handicapped children, others entrusted, in certain countries, to itinerant teachers, can all sometimes be condemned to a street existence.

Behind the drift to the cities loom still wider factors. In many developing countries, cash crops, grown for export by mechanized agribusiness, have displaced subsistence farming, leaving families with no alternative but to move to the cities, with no marketable skills or prospects of acquiring any. Disasters such as armed conflicts or drought also cause the displacement and disruption of communities.

The record of government agencies in dealing with street children is invariably poor. Most countries have an extensive safety-net of legislation to protect the child whose family is inadequate, and authorities run institutions for those in need of care if substitute families cannot be found for them through adoption and fostering. In many cases, however, such institutions serve to camouflage the real needs of the family. They have long been controversial and in practice tend to occupy an ambivalent position between the Ministry of Social Welfare and the Minister of the Interior, between protecting the child against the wide world outside and protecting society against the pre-delinquent child. The two things are very different, yet produce the same systematic exclusion and segregation.

The common lot of street children, almost everywhere, is arrest and detention in harsh circumstances. This tells us more about the real attitude of many governments to the problem than could be gathered by examining national legislation. The sad fact is that most governments are not very interested in street children. Their child-care facilities rarely make much effort to understand the deeper motivations of the child and do nothing to provide a sense of belonging.

Repressive attitudes on the part of those in authority are often compounded by bureaucracy. Ministries may be too compartmentalized, and the emergence of such new problems may point to gaps in coverage between jurisdictions. Typically, each separate ministry has far more immediate concerns on its hands than street children, and none is prepared to take overall responsibility. Departments tend to determine and shape their programmes by the available policy instruments they have, which are geared to those in families and not always flexible enough to cope with exceptions. Authorities do the minimum, and only under pressure. As for NGOs, they cannot usually fill the gap on the scale required. Having been consistently avoided, the problem has therefore to grow to huge proportions before attracting the proper attention.

Against this gloomy picture, there have always been those, in many countries, who see the issue not just in legalistic or law and order terms but above all in humanitarian terms, and who seek to provide more humane alternatives to institutional treatment. Fieldworkers, overwhelmingly from the private sector, and often with a religious background, have developed methodologies for meeting the particular needs of street children. While well aware of the deeper structural causes of the problem, they see their task as to deal firstly with the consequences, which are enough to keep them busy. They recognize that their projects can never do more than make the best of a bad job. Their calling requires seeing the young victims not as what they have become through force of circumstances, but for their own intrinsic worth.

Restoring to street children the attention of which they have been deprived requires great skill, understanding, and patience. The pioneers in the field have been visionaries passionately committed to uplifting the downtrodden and able to break through surly distrust. They are the antithesis, in every way, of the cautious bureaucrat. Whereas local authorities can supply shelter, food and other material necessities relatively easily, the crux of the matter lies rather in establishing genuine human relationships with the youngster and rebuilding his bridges with society – a task often far more difficult for the clock-watching official than for the disinterested counsellor.

Urgent cases of distress in the streets can be dealt with more thoroughly in a crisis centre, and then perhaps moved on, if there is no other solution, to a project providing residential care. The present trend, however, is rather towards the non-residential, community-based project which uses work itself, under protected conditions, as the agent of socialization. Intended for working street children who are not entirely estranged from their families, but in danger of becoming so, this formula spreads the butter thinner, and so can cater for far greater numbers. It is being actively propounded, in particular by UNICEF, as an alternative to state-run institutions.

Most of the recommendations we have made regarding the urban young in the preceding chapter apply even more to the street children. The ICIHI Sectoral Report on Street Children also contains a series of recommendations dealing with both general and specific aspects. We wish to emphasize here that the problem is too big and complex for solutions like children's homes and adoption schemes. What is required is a basic change in attitude towards street children by governments and communities. Local self-help projects involving the street children directly, as well as the old and the retired in each community, could go a longer way than expensive schemes which benefit only a few.

Besides the detailed recommendations contained in the sectoral report on street children, we suggest that governments:

* Take stock of the situation of street children, whether they are already faced with the problem or not. If it exists, they should recognize it, and seek a clearer appreciation of the actors involved and the forces at work.

* Recognize that street children as such are not delinquents, but only immediate candidates for delinquency if their needs are not met. In principle, law enforcement agencies should be used as sparingly as possible, as a heavy hand only serves to reinforce aggressiveness.

* Take steps to create a legal framework within which NGOs can operate, collect and disseminate data. Where appropriate, the confidentiality of information available to NGOs should be respected. Such a framework would recognize the responsibility of the State to protect street children.

* Encourage and support social development programmes to bring about changes of attitude regarding practices which negatively affect the institution of the family.

* Extend an umbrella of greater legality and protection to the informal sector in which many street children work. Shoe-shine boys, car washers, etc. can be given legal recognition, symbolized perhaps by a badge or a uniform. Their conditions of work can be improved and combined with nutrition programmes, informal learning, and recreation. Local authorities must take seriously the efforts by NGOs to organize them into co-operatives, and not – as has occurred in some countries – greet them with derision. The positive contribution of artisans who employ street children must be acknowledged.

The Uprooted

"There is no sorrow above the loss of a native land."

Euripides, 431 BC

Refugees and Displaced Persons

Throughout history, and in every part of the world, people have been uprooted by persecution, conflict or environmental disaster. What is unique at the present time is the massive scale and global nature of such movements. Over the last 30 years, on the average, 700 people a day have been forced to leave their homelands and to become refugees. The world's refugee population now exceeds 13 million. The number of people displaced involuntarily within their own country is much greater.

International arrangements exist to provide material assistance and protection to refugees who qualify for that status according to the universally accepted definition contained in the 1951 United Nations Convention Relating to the Status of Refugees. According to it, a person is a refugee if he is unable or unwilling to be in his own country for reasons of persecution or well-founded fear of it due to his "race, religion, nationality, membership of a particular social group or political opinion".

There are, however, tens of millions of other uprooted people in the world today whose plight is as real but whose problems are relatively ignored by the international community and the general public. We felt that it was important for our Commission to examine the different categories of these displaced people and raise public awareness of the humanitarian issues involved. Our analysis and conclusions have already been published in a Sectoral Report.*

We recognize that, in recent decades, the root causes of refugee problems have become much more complex. People

---

* See ICIHI Sectoral Report: *Refugees: Dynamics of Displacement*, Zed Books, London/New Jersey, 1986. Other language editions to appear include: Arabic, Chinese, French, Indonesian, Japanese, Russian, Spanish and Thai.

flee for a series of reasons and it is becoming increasingly difficult to distinguish clearly between refugees and non-refugees on the basis of the established criteria.

Victims of armed conflicts, for example, are not included in the definition of the 1951 Convention. Yet since World War II, the number of such conflicts, ranging from internal disturbances and civil war to undeclared wars between States, has continued to increase. Invariably, these conflicts oblige people to flee. Populations become displaced within their own countries and often spill across national borders in search of security. Understandably, some of the largest movements of refugees and displaced persons in recent years have taken place in areas of armed conflict.

Many of the world's poorer countries are locked into a vicious circle of repression and opposition. Finding that the constitutional means of expressing their opinions are limited, opposition groups turn to terrorism or guerrilla warfare. In response, the government launches a military campaign to reassert its authority and to eliminate the opposition. The civilian population, especially in rural areas, are caught between these conflicting forces and many, if they are not killed, flee for their lives.

Communal violence is one of the most frightening forms of conflict. When the members of one ethnic, religious or linguistic group clash with the neighbouring members of another, atrocities are almost inevitable. Even when governments do not have discriminatory policies, their inability to protect their own minorities or a threatened social group can indirectly cause the flight of large numbers of people.

Environmental disasters such as drought and famine are also uprooting more and more people every year. Deforestation, desertification, rapid urbanization and ineffective agricultural policies have all played a part in upsetting the delicate balance between man and his environment. The people most affected are the poor and powerless.

The development process is just as likely to uproot people as an environmental disaster. In many developing countries, land is being systematically appropriated in an attempt to fuel economic growth. Dams, highways, mines, energy pipelines and timber reserves all require large amounts of land. Planners, politicians and businessmen often regard the traditional land users as an inconvenience and a hindrance to growth. In many cases the local inhabitants are simply told to leave their land or are forcibly evicted from it.

At the same time, a growing number of people are being uprooted as a direct result of government policies to redistribute populations from over-populated to under-populated regions of the country. Sometimes these policies are a response to intractable political, economic and social problems or the perceived requirements of national security.

In the developed countries elaborate methods have been established to determine population distribution and to control the movement of migrants. Few governments in the developing countries have the resources to establish such sophisticated controls. Their administrative structures are often weak and their enforcement agencies operate with a high degree of autonomy. Decision-makers are often looking for quick solutions to complex problems. *Compulsory relocations* appear to offer a way out.

The urbanization of the developing countries has accelerated rapidly in the last forty years. Much of the increase in the urban population is a result of massive movements of people from the countryside to the towns, prompted by indebtedness, land exhaustion, and the neglect of rural areas in official development plans. In some cases, large numbers of people from the countryside flock to cities to escape armed conflicts or guerrilla activity.

Uncontrolled urban expansion places a great strain on public services in addition to creating serious social and political problems. Confronted with these problems, many governments have found it imperative to redistribute the rural population. Throughout Africa, Asia and Latin America, governments have resorted to periodic urban removal campaigns, rounding up the unemployed and underemployed, and sending them to work in the countryside.

In the rural areas themselves, people have also been uprooted. Villagization programmes have been introduced, concentrating scattered farmers into planned villages and state farms. When people are brought together, it is argued, scarce resources can be allocated more efficiently and equitably.

Serious humanitarian issues are raised by such official relocation programmes. None would deny the need for governments to take measures for containing the severe consequences of rapid urbanization and rural impoverishment. But relocation programmes have often been implemented in a coercive and poorly planned manner. What is more, they do not appear to have been particularly successful. Urban evacuees have often made their way back to the cities. Villagization programmes have failed to produce significant increases in agricultural output. Resettlement schemes have been the cause of considerable suffering, amongst both the settlers and the local populations of the resettlement areas.

Humanitarian responses to the plight of people uprooted by official relocation programmes are especially difficult to formulate. The motivations for forced relocations can often be understood, but can the methods used be endorsed? In situations where there appears to be no alternative to a controlled population movement, there is a case to be made for the involvement of external humanitarian agencies. Such a policy of constructive engagement could at least open up relocation programmes to impartial observation and ensure that they are carried out humanely and effectively. But the ambivalent attitude of many agencies to such programmes does reflect a very real dilemma: is the use of compulsion acceptable even in cases of extreme national emergency, and under what circumstances can the international community support such a policy?

The victims of *mass expulsions* are also inadequately protected and assisted by the international community. In recent years, a number of governments have attempted to resolve pressing political and economic problems by expelling unwanted sections of the population. Ethnic minorities, political dissidents, and migrant workers have been the most frequent targets of such exercises. This relatively neglected subject received the special attention of our Commission and is dealt with in greater detail later in this chapter.

The plight of all these new categories of uprooted people calls for urgent initiatives at the international level. People who are displaced within their own country are a particularly vulnerable group. Their rights are fully recognized neither in national nor international law.

We recognize the difficulty involved in regulating international law and practice in regard to matters which are essentially within the domestic jurisdiction of States. We also recognize that the internationalization of internal problems can sometimes further aggravate the situation and possibly cause more harm to the victims. It seems nonetheless feasible and desirable to elaborate internationally recognized standards of treatment for the millions who are victims of circumstances beyond their control. In situations where direct government actions contribute to displacement of large numbers of people, it should be possible to establish a code of conduct based on humanitarian principles for the guidance of governments.

The problem of refugees and displaced persons is afflicting many developing countries. There are now 25 countries in Africa, Asia and Latin America with refugee populations in excess of 80,000. In a few, the numbers run into hundreds of thousands. Most of these countries are poor. Refugee influxes and internal displacements impose a massive burden on limited government revenues and overstretched administrative structures. The burdens on ordinary people are even more significant. Impoverished newcomers compete with their local hosts for scarce resources such as food, water and fuel. Deforestation, soil erosion and a deterioration of public services are all likely to take place when an already poor area suddenly has to support a much larger population. Tension and conflict can easily arise between displaced people and host communities.

At the international level, mass displacements can reinforce political tensions and obstruct regional co-operation. Under international law, the granting of asylum is a humanitarian, non-political act. In practice, it is not always so perceived. Moreover, refugees are not only the victims of local and regional conflicts, but are sometimes also active participants in them. Governments are becoming increasingly reluctant to practise an 'open door' policy and to grant asylum generously.

The international community has tended to perceive mass displacements as an inevitable deviation from the norm. But it is now clear that refugee movements are the product of some very profound, structural problems confronting the contemporary world. The existing legal and organizational framework of refugee protection and assistance needs adjustment to this new reality.

Within the United Nations, two agencies have specific mandates to take care of defined categories of refugees: the Office of the United Nations High Commissioner for Refugees (UNHCR) which was established to protect and assist refugees and to promote permanent solutions to refugee problems and the United Nations Relief and Work Agency (UNRWA) which was established to assist and provide relief to Palestinian refugees within a defined geographic area.

When UNHCR was founded in 1951, the number of recognized refugees was less than two million. Most of them lived in the more prosperous countries of the world. Now there are over six times as many, the vast majority of them in the poorer States. Similarly the number of Palestinian refugees has continued to increase since 1948 and the problems faced by UNRWA have become more complex. A second generation of Palestinians has now been born in refugee camps in various countries of the Middle East. Hundreds of thousands of Palestinians have, thus, grown up with the despair and deprivation of camp life.

There are serious political and financial implications arising from this situation. Both UNHCR and UNRWA have had funding problems in recent years. The finances available are swallowed up by expensive relief operations and care and maintenance programmes. The inter-governmental and voluntary agencies working with refugees have, therefore, not been able to concentrate their resources on finding lasting solutions to refugee situations.

Refugee protection is weakening, as both industrialized and developing States grow tired of giving sanctuary to large numbers of distressed foreigners. A few countries have forcibly returned refugees and asylum-seekers to their own country, in clear violation of international law. Many more have introduced measures specifically designed to deter refugees from claiming asylum. Similarly, the harassment of refugees and military attacks on their settlements are growing in scale and frequency.

States cannot be forced to ratify conventions or observe

international laws designed to protect refugees. Humanitarian organizations are constrained by the realities of political power. Under certain situations they can improve the material well-being of refugees and offer them a degree of protection they might not otherwise enjoy. Exceptionally they might even help to resolve a situation which is creating refugees. But ultimately, their ability to influence the behaviour of States is quite limited. Indeed, inter-governmental organizations are often open to pressure from States in pursuit of national political or strategic interests.

There are many ways in which the protection and assistance of refugees could be strengthened. The principles of refugee law must be more widely disseminated, especially amongst the government officials and security personnel who come into contact with refugees and asylum-seekers. The specific needs of refugee women and children and of refugees who are subject to armed attacks could be recognized in United Nations declarations and special measures taken on their behalf. There is a strong case to be made for a critical re-examination of the United Nations Refugee Convention. Can it adequately meet contemporary needs and situations? Should the victims of conflict, turmoil and environmental disaster be given international legal recognition like the victims of persecution?

As far as assistance is concerned, there is a need to see whether the resources available are being equitably distributed amongst the countries giving sanctuary to large numbers of refugees. Accurate censuses of refugee populations are required, and their needs more rigorously and scientifically assessed. Governments which receive large amounts of relief aid must be encouraged to implement programmes enabling refugee communities to become self-sufficient. The resilience and innovative ability of refugees is often underestimated by aid agencies. The fact is that an overwhelming majority of refugees survive without international aid. They integrate into the new society more easily on their own in the developing countries. Such 'spontaneous integration' should be encouraged and facilitated through appropriate projects which take fully into account local conditions and traditions.

In recent decades, ambitious schemes of resettlement of refugees in countries outside their region have been implemented. While the generosity of receiving countries is commendable, it is important that resettlement within the region rather than across the continents is encouraged. Instead of spending vast sums to integrate refugees in an entirely alien social environment, donors would do well to assist more generously countries within the region to assimilate them.

Most refugees would like to go home, but will not do so until the conditions which prompted them to leave have changed. In many cases, they are deterred from returning by the daunting prospect of establishing a livelihood and reintegrating into their own society. External assistance has a vital role to play in promoting the option of voluntary repatriation. The assistance currently given to returnees is often inadequate. Food aid, for example, is provided for a very limited period. Much more ambitious programmes, designed to rehabilitate the infrastructure of returnee areas and to provide new income-earning opportunities, are called for. With aid agency personnel stationed in these areas for an adequate period of time, the security of returnees would also be reinforced.

The circumstances which force people to abandon their homes and which prompt governments to uproot their citizens do not spring up overnight. They develop gradually and are, therefore, foreseeable. Yet the international community has hitherto failed to establish an effective early warning system which would enable contingency planning and anticipatory action to be taken.

We need to know much more about the dynamics of mass displacement. On the basis of that knowledge, the international community should be able to establish a means of collecting, sifting and analysing information relevant to potential refugee movements. Given the very rapid development of communications and computer technology, a new early warning facility should have a substantial forecasting potential.

At the same time, we must recognize that preventive and anticipatory action is more often obstructed by political than technical obstacles. Governments have the ultimate responsibility for the actions, or failures to act, that cause refugee movements.

In seeking change at the political and governmental levels, the role of the public cannot be over-emphasized. Throughout the world, ordinary men and women have demonstrated in recent years their concern for the victims of famine in Africa. Such concern must be directed, not simply at the collection of money for relief, but at the governments and decision-makers who shape the policies which create or aggravate refugee problems instead of solving them.

In conclusion, we wish to emphasize the need for elaborating international humanitarian standards and strengthening the assistance network at national and international level for those groups of uprooted persons who do not clearly fall within the category of refugees as defined by existing international instruments. We recognize that this relatively unexplored field does not lend itself easily to definitive recommendations and suggestions without a more thorough study. We urge governments, inter-governmental agencies and non-governmental organizations, as well as scholars and experts to undertake such studies and to look into practical ways and means to alleviate suffering and promote solutions to the problems. There are now tens of millions of internally and externally displaced persons and their numbers may well increase if timely action is not taken.

We are of the opinion, in so far as refugees as defined by existing instruments are concerned, that, in the field of protection:

* It is essential to elaborate further the concept and State practice relating to asylum. The international community must support this process giving positive expression to the notions of burden-sharing and human solidarity. States should be dissuaded from introducing measures designed to deter individuals from seeking asylum. Likewise, it is essential that governments deal with asylum applications quickly, thoroughly and in a context where humanitarianism prevails over political considerations. The inter- and non-governmental agencies concerned have a vital role to play in assisting governments in this regard and in exerting pressure when humanitarian principles are not fully respected.

* A set of minimum humanitarian standards applicable to refugees and asylum-seekers should be developed and the international agencies should monitor and encourage their observance by governments and local communities.

* The physical security of refugees in situations of conflict must be strengthened by governments and the international agencies should play an active supervisory role.

* International humanitarian agencies must enjoy free access to refugees and in situations of tension or conflict the possibility of stationing impartial 'humanitarian observers' should be explored.

Regarding material assistance, we are of the opinion that:

* Available sources must be equitably distributed among the countries receiving large numbers of refugees, and objective humanitarian rather than political criteria should be applied by donors.

* Accurate censuses of refugee populations are required and their needs should be more precisely assessed.

* Emergency relief assistance should be provided for a pre-determined and limited period and income-generating projects as well as assistance measures designed to promote self-sufficiency should be encouraged.

* The concept of refugee camps and rural settlement needs to be radically reviewed. Beyond the emergency period when they are required, camps have serious disadvantages. They rarely become self-sufficient. They also produce social tensions and constitute 'human islands' which isolate refugees from their local hosts while creating open-ended dependency upon external assistance.

* Criteria of material aid to refugees should be standardized in terms of nutrition, health care and other subsistence items. Donors should provide aid which corresponds to real, identified needs as well as the habits and traditions of the recipients.

In terms of durable solutions, we firmly believe that:

* Voluntary repatriation, as the most suitable solution, calls for a more vigorous approach on the part of international organizations and governments. While respecting scrupulously the voluntary character of repatriation, efforts should be made to create a climate more conducive to return. It is important in this connection to strengthen aid programmes for returnees. Such programmes should be of longer duration than a few months and should be designed to promote self-sufficiency.

★ In the case of local settlement, the concept of 'spontaneous integration' or self-settlement needs greater attention and encouragement than has hitherto been accorded to it. It is the preferred option of a majority of refugees and calls for better understanding of local conditions by the aid agencies. They should call on experts possessing knowledge of the customs, habits, traditions and historical background of refugees and local host communities, in order to develop appropriate assistance projects to encourage and facilitate self-settlement.

★ Finally, with regard to the resettlement of refugees in a third country, the possibilities of resettlement within the region or the continent should be vigorously pursued. Where necessary, donors should provide extra assistance to the countries and the local communities to facilitate integration and self-sufficiency of refugees. Inter-continental migration should be pursued only when all possibilities of resettlement within the region have been fully explored and exhausted.

Statelessness*

"Citizenship is man's basic right for it is nothing less than the right to have rights."

Earl Warren, 1958

In a world where the nation state assumes increasing importance, nationality is an essential attribute of a person's material and moral well-being. Normally every individual has a nationality, and one only. In reality, some people have several nationalities, while others – much more numerous – have none. They are stateless. No State considers them as one of its own. There are hundreds of thousands of people in this predicament spread across the globe, although exact figures are difficult to determine. The subject of statelessness has received little detailed attention from international organizations.

Some people are born stateless, others become stateless in the course of their lifetime. Certain countries confer nationality

---

* ICIHI Sectoral Report to be published in 1988.

according to the principle of birth within national boundaries (*jus soli*), others confer it according to filiation (*jus sanguinis*). With regard to statelessness after birth, there may be several causes. An individual may lose his or her nationality without acquiring a new one as a result of an extended stay abroad, or due to the ceding of territory, or for some perceived disloyalty, or as a punishment, or simply through marriage to someone of a different nationality. In this last case, it is usually women who lose their nationality. From a legal point of view, statelessness may be considered as the faulty expression of national legislations on the question of nationality and the principle by which the law of each State fixes the acquisition, attribution or loss of nationality.

Statelessness is not merely a legal problem. It is also a consequence of migrations, of movements of population, of forced exodus and of various forms of persecution. The frequency and growing magnitude of these problems in recent years explains, to a large extent, the renewed interest in statelessness, and particularly in de facto statelessness.

De facto stateless people, as distinct from de jure stateless people, do theoretically have a nationality. But they have lost all real links with their country of origin and no longer have its protection, either because the country in question refuses to afford assistance and protection, or because the people in question have renounced it. Their situation is similar to that of refugees who, while keeping their nationality, no longer benefit from the effective protection of their State. Stateless people are not, however, all refugees, and, conversely, refugees are not all stateless. In practice, the distinction between de jure and de facto statelessness is not always evident and this has sometimes led to the use of the terms 'de jure non-protected persons' and 'de facto non-protected persons', or 'technically stateless persons' and 'politically stateless people', in order to demonstrate the origin of non-protection.

As de facto stateless persons, there are also those who have never had a nationality. In particular, the case of many Palestinians serves as illustration. There are also nomads and gypsies who live on the fringes of the nation state and who, as it were, embrace statelessness voluntarily. Their situation raises particular problems which the Council of Europe, for example, is trying to solve. Its recommendation of 1983 calls on States to retain certain criteria, such as the country of origin of immediate family or of frequent periods of residence, in order to facilitate their membership of a State and to allow them to travel freely.

From a humanitarian point of view, statelessness, whether de jure or de facto, is a major preoccupation. The stateless are part of those unwanted people who are refused right of entry to countries or who are turned back at borders according to political or economic circumstances. If they are taken in, they often live in uncertainty for many years. Statelessness is frequently transmitted from one generation to another. Nationality is not only the right to a passport and material advantages. It also confers upon the individual an identity and the sense of belonging to a community – elements without which a person remains vulnerable and uprooted.

As a result of events during the inter-war years and the Second World War, the Universal Declaration of Human Rights proclaimed the right to a nationality as a fundamental human right. Article 15 states:

1. Everyone has the right to a nationality.

2. No-one shall be arbitrarily deprived of his nationality, nor denied the right to change his nationality.

But much effort is still required before this right is fully recognized. In recent decades, the international community became aware of the problem of stateless people at the same time as it was preoccupied with the fate of refugees. However, the two issues were dealt with separately by the United Nations. It is now becoming increasingly apparent that, in practice, the stateless are less protected than refugees.

The 1954 Convention of the United Nations relating to the Status of Stateless Persons, formulated along the same lines as the 1951 Convention relating to the Status of Refugees, confers a special status on the stateless and guarantees them minimum standards of treatment. Stateless persons are thus granted the same rights as nationals in certain areas: the right of access to courts of law, industrial and intellectual property, education, assistance and social security. For other rights and activities, they should be granted treatment no less favourable than generally accorded to aliens as regards movable and immovable property, the right of association, the right to engage in wage-earning or unsalaried employment, the right to practise a liberal profession, the right to housing, education up to and beyond primary level, and freedom of movement. The Convention also requests States to issue to stateless persons identity papers and travel documents and to take measures to facilitate their assimilation and naturalization.

The treatment of stateless persons and refugees has many similarities. There are, however, certain differences which make statelessness a less advantageous situation than that of refugees. In the event of illegal entry or presence, only refugees are exempt from penalties. They are also guaranteed freedom from expulsion or forcible return to a country where they risk being persecuted. However, the 1954 Convention offers no more than a statutory arrangement for stateless persons. It does not offer a definitive solution. It does not look into the problem of nationality which is, after all, the only means to ensure true and lasting integration of the stateless into a national community.

In this sense, the 1961 Convention on the Reduction of Statelessness took a step forward by attacking the problem at its source. Stateless children should be granted the nationality of the State in whose territory they are born. This would avoid perpetuating statelessness from one generation to the next. If all countries were to conform to this principle, namely that of *jus soli*, there would be far fewer stateless persons. But this is hardly the case. Many countries apply the rule of *jus sanguinis*. They ensured that their own interests were preserved in the 1961 Convention. The co-existence of both principles weakens the efficacy of the Convention in relation to its avowed aim.

The Convention also seeks to avoid cases of statelessness which are the result of voluntary omission, of a change in civil status, of the stripping of nationality or of the transfer of territorial sovereignty. The Convention essentially ensures that no person shall lose his or her nationality without a guarantee of acquiring another. However, even here, the prerogatives of sovereignty have been assuaged, and exceptions introduced which largely reduce the scope of the principles in question. This is certainly the case of persons who may lose their nationality as a result of extended residence abroad. Others may be deprived of nationality if, for example, they represent 'a serious threat' to the 'essential interests' of the State. These notions are not spelt out in more detail, and their interpretation often results in injustice and arbitrary measures.

De facto statelessness has been particularly overlooked in international conventions. Protection under the 1954 Convention is only aimed at people who have obtained status as stateless persons. Other than those who also have refugee status, and thereby enjoy more favourable conditions, the majority of de facto stateless persons are without protection. Even in war time when the number of refugees and stateless persons increases, the 1977 Geneva Protocols expressly qualify as protected persons only those stateless persons considered as such before the outbreak of hostilities, namely the de jure stateless.

A recommendation included in the Final Act of the Conference on the Status of Stateless Persons invites the Contracting States to extend the treatment accorded by the Convention to de facto stateless persons who have renounced the protection of their own State. Among the resolutions included in the Final Act of the Conference on the Reduction of Statelessness is one which recommends that persons who are stateless de facto should be treated as stateless de jure to enable them to acquire an effective nationality. But these are only recommendations which are in no way binding upon States.

Despite numerous compromises and concessions, the Conventions on Statelessness have not received the number of ratifications one might have hoped for: only 35 States have ratified the 1954 Convention and 13 that of 1961.

To the weakness of standard-setting, one must add negligence by existing institutions. Stateless persons are almost alone therefore when facing the State. They frequently leave their country without any resources or valid identity papers. They may either be forcibly returned, or admitted temporarily and then rejected and escorted to the frontier. They may be mistreated – without any international organization offering assistance. The Convention relating to the Status of Refugees was able to benefit from the establishment of the Office of the United Nations High Commissioner for Refugees (UNHCR) which was entrusted with its supervision and application. UNHCR has the mandate to assist refugees, ensure their legal protection and follow up with the authorities of host countries. There are no such mechanisms for stateless persons.

The 1961 Convention did foresee the establishment within the framework of the United Nations of a body to which persons claiming the benefit of the Convention might apply. UNHCR was so designated by the UN General Assembly (Resolution 3274 (XXIX) of 10 December 1974 and Resolution 31/36 of 30 November 1976). But no mention is made of UNHCR's competence with regard to the application of the 1954 Convention and to measures of assistance towards those who have not yet been deemed stateless persons. Moreover, UNHCR, which could in practice go beyond conventional limits, has remained somewhat indifferent when it comes to the fate of the stateless. The term stateless person hardly ever appears in UNHCR publications – a fact which, together with the doctrinal vacuum in this particular area, only serves to heighten general indifference towards a problem which should, rather, inspire in human terms the same compassion as that shown to refugees.

The solutions provided so far by the international community with regard to the problem of statelessness have been found wanting and inefficient. They have been formulated more from the point of view of a State's prerogatives and sovereignty than of individual human rights. It is this imbalance which today requires correction through a new approach which takes into account the many dimensions of the problem. Action must be aimed at prevention and elimination.

With regard to nationality, the law needs to be strengthened and better defined. The 1961 Convention does not express an international consensus. Few States (only 35 of them) participated in the Conference and only 13 have ratified the Convention. The elaboration of a new instrument might allow the emergence of a consensus and a new standard which, in any case, would serve to influence national legislation.

The 1961 Convention was a compromise between those countries which, in turn, supported either *jus soli* or *jus sanguinis*. Ideally, any future international instrument should go beyond compromises to a comprehensive approach to the elimination of statelessness. It would be advisable, for example, to adopt a single criterion for the acquisition of nationality: that of *jus soli*. The 1969 American Convention on Human Rights, for example, recognizes the right of any person to acquire the nationality of the State in whose territory he or she was born.

The ability to deprive a citizen of nationality should be forbidden absolutely if it leads to statelessness. There are other measures that can be taken against those who go against national interests. A State should not turn away its own citizens, or ex-citizens who have no other nationality.

In the case of ceding of territory, States must ensure that the inhabitants do not become stateless. They might give the inhabitants, for example, the right to choose between the nationality of the successor or the predecessor State.

The best way to eliminate statelessness is to allow stateless persons to acquire a nationality. States should envisage advantageous ways of naturalization and distinguish them from those usually offered to foreigners. In the event of a country of residence not granting its nationality to a stateless person, the United Nations should look into ways and means to resolve the problem. It is up to the United Nations to initiate and encourage the international community to be more sensitive to the problem of statelessness.

Mechanisms to protect and assist stateless persons should be established urgently. It is possible, for example, to envisage, through a protocol to the 1954 Convention, the creation of a High Commissioner for Stateless Persons. However, it would be more appropriate to confer this task upon UNHCR. This would be a way not only of gaining from its experience in the field of protection, but of saving time, money and energy. UNHCR already has been given by the UN General Assembly the functions foreseen in the 1961 Convention. It should also monitor the application of the 1954 Convention. The mandate of UNHCR is sufficiently flexible. In the same way that it is charged with the task of protecting refugees and displaced persons who do not fall under the definition of the 1951 Convention, it should be empowered to extend its activities to all stateless persons, de jure or de facto. It is important to recall

The Victims

in this connection that UNHCR has on-going activities not only in countries which are party to the Convention, but also in many which have not ratified it.

We believe it would be helpful if UNHCR could assume the following tasks:

* Promote the ratification of international Conventions relating to statelessness.

* Monitor the application of Conventions and report to the General Assembly on the state of application of Conventions and of its activities in favour of stateless persons.

* Collect all possible information concerning stateless persons, their number and whereabouts. The task should be all the easier in that UNHCR already undertakes this for refugees and that, within national administrations, it is often the same department which deals with refugees and stateless persons.

* Co-operate with governments with a view to improving the condition of stateless persons and reduce their number through the adoption of permanent solutions, through appropriate inter-governmental agreements.

* Assist stateless persons in administrative matters and inform them of their rights.

* Raise public awareness of the problems of stateless persons and promote the reduction and elimination of statelessness.

* Include the needs of stateless persons in its public information and fund-raising activities.

The 1961 Convention foresees the jurisdiction of the International Court of Justice in the event of disputes concerning the interpretation or application of the Convention. But the prerogative of seizing the Court is reserved for States. It would appear timely to set up an international authority to which stateless persons themselves could apply in order to uphold their rights. Nationality is not a simple affair of state. It is also a human right.

Statelessness is a source of political and socio-economic tension which affects the country of origin, the country of residence and neighbouring countries. Regional organizations should become more involved in the problem and contribute to its solution through initiatives adapted to local conditions. Regional mechanisms to control human rights could also be used to ensure respect for the right of every individual to a nationality and related rights such as that of choosing one's place of residence, of freely entering one's own country, or of not being expelled from it.

Mass Expulsions*

"Everyone is quick to blame the foreigner."

Aeschylus, 463 BC

Mass expulsions of foreigners as well as unwanted nationals are not just a modern phenomenon. Between the 15th and 18th centuries, religious turmoil in Europe led to the exclusion of minority groups such as French Protestants, Spanish Muslims and Austrian Jews. In the first half of this century, territorial realignments and the growth of nationalism resulted in widespread displacements of populations. After the Second World War, the redrawing of the political map in Europe and the Middle East, and the process of decolonization in other parts of the world, inevitably produced a succession of mass expulsions. Most recently, developing countries confronted with intractable economic and political problems have resorted to the expulsion of 'scapegoat' groups, such as refugees, ethnic minorities and illegal immigrant workers.

Despite the long history of mass expulsions, which have meant deprivation and death for hundreds of thousands of people and caused major social, economic and political upheavals, very little has been done at the international or even regional level to tackle the issue. There is no organization, either within or outside the United Nations system, with a specific mandate to deal with the problem. There has been no concerted attempt to formulate an international instrument or even a code of conduct to prevent or regulate mass expulsions.

---

* ICIHI Sectoral Report to be published in 1988.

Although the expulsion of undesirable foreign individuals is considered to be within the sovereign legal prerogative of States, a number of jurists agree that *mass* expulsions of nationals or aliens can be considered unlawful under international law: they are arbitrary in their effect, they violate human rights, and cause unnecessary hardship to large numbers of innocent and vulnerable people. Of course, the governments which implement mass expulsions claim that they have a right to do so.

Economic justifications are commonly uppermost in official statements on this issue. Migrant workers from developing countries, perhaps the most regular victims of mass expulsions in recent years, are blamed for taking jobs that should be held by a country's own citizens. It is argued that migrant workers, especially those who enter a country in an irregular way, place undue pressure on public services in times of austerity, and aggravate balance of payments crises by sending remittances back to their own country.

Some migratory movements result in the establishment of settled alien communities. Business communities, sometimes termed 'middlemen minorities', have repeatedly been subject to expulsion. These communities commonly dominate the trading and commercial sector of their adopted country, and are set apart from the rest of the population by their race, religion or nationality. They usually retain an orientation towards their country of origin which, combined with their economic success, isolates them from the host community and renders them liable to charges of disloyalty and dishonesty.

Other categories of migrants have been subject to expulsion in recent years, although not in such great numbers as migrant labourers and settled traders and entrepreneurs. Groups of environmental refugees, forced to flee disasters such as floods, earthquakes, drought and famine, have occasionally been expelled from States which claim not to have the resources to care for large numbers of distressed foreigners. Even genuine refugees, victims of conflict or persecution, have been subject to mass expulsions from countries which regard them as an economic or political liability. In many recent cases of mass expulsion, economic justifications have been advanced by governments to disguise their real, political motives.

Four related sets of political motives for mass expulsion can be identified, in which both domestic and international considerations feature. First, expulsions result from a desire to find convenient scapegoats for a government's policy failures. Second, they have been instigated during periods of political unrest, when minority groups represent a perceived threat to national security. Third, such minorities are vulnerable in the run-up to elections, when ruling parties attempt to maintain power by making dramatic populist gestures. Finally, expulsions are used in the course of international disputes, to humiliate or create practical problems for rival States.

But experience suggests that mass expulsions cause a great deal of needless suffering and seldom achieve their intended or stated objectives. In fact, they frequently prove to be counter-productive.

Economic dislocation is common in the wake of large-scale expulsions. The departure of migrant workers can leave major gaps in the labour market without significantly reducing unemployment amongst nationals. The disruption of commerce may also occur, especially in countries where expelled minorities have special skills or play an important role in the trading or manufacturing sectors.

Expulsions can easily provoke conflict between neighbouring States, impeding efforts to encourage regional co-operation. There is a constant danger that a State receiving large numbers of expellees will take reprisals, leading to a further deterioration of relations, increased spending on defence, and a greater risk of military conflict.

Receiving States are confronted with enormous problems on account of mass expulsions. In the short term, they have to arrange for the reception and rehabilitation of the expellees, who often arrive without resources and in a state of destitution. In the longer term, receiving States have to deal with the prospect of increased unemployment, pressure on public resources and competition for land. The return of disappointed and frustrated emigrants is also a source of social and political frictions, especially when they have been accustomed to a higher standard of living in another country. But it would be misleading to suggest that the consequences of mass expulsion are inevitably negative, especially in the longer term. Critics of migrant labour systems have long argued that the skills and energy of migrant workers should be used productively at home rather than contributing to growth abroad.

Although there is no specific international mechanism to deal with the problem of mass expulsions, it would not be desirable to establish a new office or to revise the mandate of an existing agency to fill the gap. However, it would be appropriate to designate an agency to forecast mass expulsions, monitor them and promote preventive measures. Despite its specific mandate and limited means, the United Nations Disaster Relief Office (UNDRO) has been considered the appropriate inter-governmental body in the United Nations system. Of course, other agencies – UNICEF, the World Food Programme, the International Labour Office and the United Nations High Commissioner for Refugees – have an important role to play, as does the Red Cross and the voluntary agencies. Co-ordination between them and collective assistance to the designated body would be vital.

International legal responses must also be strengthened. The expulsion of nationals constitutes an unlawful act. As for foreign nationals, their mass expulsion, as distinguished from expulsion of individuals, should be subject to closer international scrutiny. The onus is clearly on the expelling State to avoid such action if possible, to justify the instigation of expulsions when they take place, and to give due regard to the human rights of the group targeted for expulsion. Some progress has recently been made in this direction. In 1986, the International Law Association produced a Declaration of Principles of International Law on Mass Expulsion, which could serve as a useful basis for further discussion and action by the international community.

Some forms of mass expulsion may prove difficult to eliminate. While States continue to make use of disappearances, detention without trial and torture, they are unlikely to eschew the relatively mild remedy of mass expulsions in their attempt to solve difficult political and economic problems.

But like so many other forms of mass displacement, the conditions which lead States to implement mass expulsions do not spring up overnight. A government which pursues a laissez-faire immigration policy during a period of economic growth cannot expect large numbers of migrant workers to pack their bags and leave voluntarily as soon as recession sets in. A country which benefits from the entrepreneurial activities of a minority group cannot expect to deprive that group of its economic and political influence. States must therefore be sensitized to the need for foresight, long-term planning and due respect for the rights of minorities whether they be foreign or national.

The international community must look for ways of anticipating and preventing mass expulsions. The United Nations system in particular has a major role to play.

In this context, we are of the view that it would be useful if the United Nations would:

* ★ Utilize its fact-finding role to investigate and clarify the issues involved in potential mass expulsion situations.

* ★ Monitor mass expulsions and ensure respect for fundamental human rights.

* ★ Use its 'good offices' to relieve tensions between the expelling and receiving State.

* ★ Help to co-ordinate the activities of governmental, inter-governmental and voluntary agencies both before and after a relief programme has become necessary.

We urge the international community to support the United Nations in this task by providing the assistance required for the victims of mass expulsions to be returned to and resettled in the receiving State in conditions of safety and dignity.

We believe that the protection of people subjected to mass expulsions could be enhanced by developing a legal instrument or a set of principles governing their treatment. The 1986 Declaration of Principles of International Law on Mass Expulsion, of the International Law Association just mentioned, could provide a suitable starting point. Recognizing that mass expulsions can, in certain circumstances, be considered lawful, the international community should take full account of Principle 17 of this Declaration which states: 'Mass expulsion of aliens . . . must not be arbitrary or discriminatory in its application, or serve as a pretext for genocide, confiscation of property or reprisal. The power of expulsion must be exercised in conformity with the principles of good faith, proportionality and justifiability, with due regard to the basic rights of the individuals concerned.'

The Neglected

Indigenous Peoples*

"It is natural anywhere that people like their own kind, but it is not necessarily natural that their fondness for their own kind should lead them to the subjection of whole groups of other people not like them."

Pearl S. Buck, 1943

From the polar reaches of Scandinavia to the equatorial forests of Brazil, from the deserts of Australia to the mountains of India, indigenous peoples are linked by their common needs and problems. There are 200 million of them, living on all continents, both in rich as well as poor countries. They have a common cause which transcends ideological and national frontiers and demands humanitarian action.

Whether they are called indigenous, autochthonous or tribal people, First Nations or Fourth World, there is a growing awareness about these peoples. They are the descendants of populations who inhabited a territory at the time when persons of a different culture or ethnic origin arrived there from elsewhere and, by conquest or settlement, reduced them to a non-dominant or colonial condition.

Indigenous peoples are often nomadic herders, hunters, or shifting cultivators living in sparsely populated regions of the world – in forests, deserts or mountains. There they have co-existed with the environment without harming it and they depend upon it for their livelihood and culture. Even though

---

* ICIHI Sectoral Report: *Indigenous Peoples: A Global Quest for Justice*, Zed Books, London/New Jersey, 1987. Also to be published in: Filipino, French, Indonesian, Japanese, Portuguese, Quechua and Spanish.

many of them are self-sufficient, their traditional economic activities and physical isolation have made them particularly vulnerable to powerful political and economic forces encroaching on their societies. Not all indigenous peoples, however, are isolated herders, hunters or cultivators. Increasingly they live and work in cities and relate in varying degrees to the dominant society. Notwithstanding their diversity and geographic distance, indigenous peoples share common historical experiences and problems.

Indigenous peoples, like oppressed minorities, are subjected to discrimination sometimes bordering on racism. Their languages, religions and cultures are often ridiculed as 'primitive' by the dominant social groups. Degrading racial stereotypes directed towards indigenous peoples circulate unchallenged and are sometimes encouraged by governments. Many are excluded from government and senior professional jobs. A higher proportion of indigenous peoples in all countries are unemployed and, if working, employed in low-income jobs. Pressures of modernization and development have made them more vulnerable, socially and physically. They suffer comparatively poor health and have limited access to health care services. They are victims of discrimination in housing and education. When they do have access to education, it is normally in the official language of the country and unrelated to indigenous life and culture. Indigenous peoples are invariably placed last in national hierarchies whether they form a majority of the population, as they do in Guatemala and Bolivia, or a small minority as they do in Brazil and Finland.

At the core of indigenous culture is their relationship with the land. They share a world view which incorporates as its fundamental principle a custodial attitude to land and its natural resources. Indigenous peoples regard the land as a living entity entrusted to them for safe-keeping and for passing on intact to future generations. It is anathema to indigenous peoples that land can be treated as a commodity, to be bought and sold, exploited and abandoned. Governments, however, tend to regard indigenous values and farming methods as outdated and inappropriate in the modern world even though the agricultural practices of indigenous peoples have proved the most successful and environmentally sound form of land usage

121

in fragile ecological systems.

In recent decades, the traditional territories of indigenous peoples have been subjected increasingly to incursions. An ever-growing demand, particularly from industrial nations, for natural resources has spurred a global search for untapped reserves. Once thought of as barren wastelands of little economic value, the unexploited territories of indigenous peoples have been identified as areas of abundant timber, minerals, petroleum and water. In the name of development, forests are cleared, the earth is mined, and waterways are dammed, rendering indigenous lands uninhabitable and forcing the occupants to leave. Often without clear legal title in the modern sense to the land they occupy, and with little political influence, indigenous peoples are unable to stop these incursions. Thus their alienation from the land which began with invasions and colonization has continued unabated.

The injustice of the exploitation of indigenous peoples' land is also clear from the fact that, despite the enormous wealth it generates, little is returned to them. Even where governments have guaranteed reserves for indigenous peoples, these have generally not included rights to the natural resources of the land. In some countries there may be a limited protection of sites of religious or cultural importance, but governments retain the final authority over whether resources will be extracted from the land and the conditions which will apply. And because of indigenous peoples' precarious land rights, fair compensation for their land and its resources has not been forthcoming from governments and transnational corporations.

Invasions of indigenous peoples' land are made in the name of economic development and the will of the majority, but they rarely bring higher standards of living and other material benefits to the inhabitants themselves. Instead, national development, as presently imposed on them, is often causing landlessness, impoverishment and long-term degradation of the environment on which they depend. Adequate social and environmental impact studies to assess the likely effects of development projects on indigenous peoples are rarely conducted. Benefits could accrue if they were consulted by the development planners and given some control over the implementation of major projects. But in most cases, they are excluded from the development process.

Historically, the most extensive use of indigenous peoples' land has been government-sponsored colonization programmes. These open the territories of indigenous peoples to poor or landless peasants from more densely populated areas, turning indigenous peoples into minorities in their own territories. Moreover, large numbers of people unfamiliar with the often fragile environment where indigenous peoples live, can irreparably damage the land for all. Recent colonization programmes, under the guise of economic development, have attracted substantial funding from multilateral development banks. However, they have been largely unsuccessful because they failed to take into account the practical knowledge and wisdom that indigenous peoples have gained through the generations. Unsuitable development measures are often blindly imposed without consulting the traditional owners. Consequently, both resettled peasants and indigenous peoples are made victims of preventable policy mistakes.

Indigenous peoples are also victims of military activities and defence strategies in a number of countries. Their lands are used for military exercises, nuclear and other weapons tests and for the stationing of bases. These activities have undermined indigenous economies, degraded the environment, forced them to move in many cases, and caused grave hazards to their health. Seccessionist movements, sometimes exacerbated by arbitrary boundaries established by colonial powers or by refusal of States to grant autonomy to indigenous peoples, have also brought about war and violence. Indigenous territories have often suffered internal colonization at the hands of governments which fear secessionist threats. In other cases, genocidal solutions have been used by many governments to resolve what is essentially a humanitarian issue. Whole communities of indigenous people have been brutally massacred and hundreds of thousands have fled their homelands to escape barbarous killings by national armed forces. Peoples straddling frontiers are particularly vulnerable to inter-state or civil conflict.

Often when indigenous people are forced to leave their land, they move to cities in search of work. But when they leave their largely self-sufficient and economically self-reliant traditional communities, they are profoundly transformed. Upon arrival in the cities, they experience severe housing problems and settle in unhealthy, overcrowded slums and shanty towns. Endemic unemployment is the norm. Those who find no work often survive through petty crime, drug pushing and prostitution. Extended family structures break down and leave the individual isolated. Alcoholism and high suicide rates follow. To be 'assimilated' into the urban society in this negative way is nothing short of ethnocide because it denies to the indigenous people the right to enjoy, develop and disseminate their own culture and language. Assimilation on these terms has been the fate of many millions of indigenous peoples since colonization began and continues to be a threat to millions more.

In reaction to the hardships they face, an international movement of indigenous peoples has emerged to defend their rights and promote their interests. They demand tangible respect for their land rights, natural resources, cultures, languages and customs as fundamental human rights. They call for an end to persecution and victimization arising from militarization and acts of ethnocide and genocide. Indigenous peoples are not opposed to economic development to promote global welfare if it brings benefits to their communities and does not destroy the environment. However, there is no effective legislation and mechanisms in place to protect them at the national and international level. Consequently, their welfare and, indeed, survival depend not only on their own struggle but also upon the support of all those individuals, institutions and governments, that understand and promote their humanitarian cause.

Our views and suggestions relating to the various issues affecting indigenous peoples are reflected in the Sectoral Report which has already been published. The main recommendations, for action at different levels, are summarized below:

At the national level, we urge governments:

* To recognize and promote respect for the populations, territories and institutions of indigenous peoples. They should be guaranteed the right to manage their own affairs and to

determine their own future, while enjoying equal rights in the affairs of the State. The customs and traditions of indigenous peoples should be respected and effectively protected and promoted. They should have the right to determine their own status as indigenous people and play the decisive role in terms of their own social organization and culture as well as development.

* To guarantee to indigenous peoples rights to their traditional territories and natural resources. In cases where land has been taken away without their consent, it should be returned or adequately compensated for. Treaties and agreements between indigenous peoples and States, or between States affecting indigenous peoples, should be honoured by governments. Relocation of indigenous peoples or settlement in their territories should take place only with their full and informed consent.

* To combat discrimination against indigenous communities and to educate the general public in order to create support for governmental action in favour of indigenous peoples' rights and welfare. In this regard, review and revision of national histories and textbooks, taking into account the views of the indigenous population, must be a priority.

* To increase funding for indigenous social services and education to reach, at least, the minimum level of the rest of the population. Indigenous peoples should be enabled to manage these services in accordance with their own customs and traditions. Governments should also provide funds for indigenous peoples to maintain legal and technical expertise of their own choice to assist in their negotiations with the government, with corporations, and others. Any government bodies established to promote the interests of indigenous peoples should be autonomous, include indigenous representatives, and have full authority to intervene effectively on their behalf.

* To contribute generously to the newly established United Nations Voluntary Fund for Indigenous Populations and take all necessary measures to ensure their representation in the relevant international forums.

In the field of development, we recommend that:

* Governments, development banks and transnational corporations consult fully with indigenous peoples before projects are

initiated in their territories. Comprehensive social and environmental impact studies should be undertaken with the collaboration of indigenous peoples before any development project is approved, funded or implemented. These studies should indicate the additional cost estimates of the project on the basis of profit-sharing arrangements with the indigenous community, land reclamation, training and employment programmes, and various forms of compensation due to the community.

* Multinational development banks ensure that indigenous peoples are in favour of and support the development projects they finance. They should adopt a code of conduct, in co-operation with indigenous representatives, governing the conditions for loans relating to indigenous peoples' lands and lives. Development banks should accept the principle of active participation by indigenous peoples in resource development projects, including in particular the planning and implementation process.

* The World Bank, with the collaboration of indigenous peoples, revise its policy statement on tribal peoples so that existing ambiguities are removed.

* Transnational corporations draft a code of conduct with indigenous representatives to govern projects they conduct on or which affect their land. This would include indigenous approval, profit-sharing, land restoration and proper compensation for loss of land and resources. Such a code of conduct should ensure local preferential hiring and job training.

* Corporations both commercial and non-profit, including those of indigenous peoples, contribute generously to the United Nations Voluntary Fund for Indigenous Populations.

At the international level, we call upon:

* The International Labour Organization to make every effort to meet its timetable to revise its Indigenous Populations Convention (107) by 1989, and incorporate the recommendations it has received from indigenous representatives and other experts. The greatest number of States should promptly ratify and implement the revised Convention. The ILO should devise a mechanism for the inclusion of indigenous representatives, both in the revision process and for monitoring implementation of the Convention. In order that the work of revision and monitoring

of the revised Convention be effective, human and financial resources should be increased.

* The Working Group on Indigenous Populations of the United Nations Sub-Commission on Prevention of Discrimination and Protection of Minorities to accelerate its task of preparing a draft declaration of indigenous peoples' rights. It should be enabled to devote more time to review developments. It should also hold periodic meetings in countries or locations of indigenous communities. Its allocated financial and human resources should be increased substantially.

* The newly established United Nations Voluntary Fund for Indigenous Populations to broaden its mandate to enable it to fund the travel of indigenous representatives to a range of relevant international meetings in addition to the UN Working Group's annual meeting in Geneva.

* The international agencies such as UNESCO, UNEP, UNCTAD, UNIDO, UNICEF, UNHCR, WHO, FAO, UNRISD, UNITAR, as well as regional inter-governmental organizations, to include the issues of indigenous populations in their agendas and programmes. Indigenous professionals should be recruited to help in the elaboration and implementation of programmes.

* All relevant committees of the United Nations to include discussion of indigenous issues. For example, the Committee on Transnational Corporations should include the effect of their activities on indigenous lands in its development of a code of conduct; the Committee on Disarmament should examine the question of effects of military activities on the lives and lands of indigenous peoples.

For immediate action, we are of the opinion that:

* Recourse procedures must be established within the United Nations to examine threats to the survival and well-being of indigenous peoples. An international ombudsman, under the United Nations aegis, could help monitor such situations. Such a person, designated by the United Nations Secretary-General on the basis of objectivity and impartiality and internationally recognized experience and expertise, should report to the General Assembly, through the Secretary-General, all crisis situations affecting indigenous peoples, including armed conflicts, forced relocations, ethnocide and genocide.

* As recommended by the United Nations Sub-Commission Special Rapporteur on the Problem of Discrimination against Indigenous Populations, an official study should be made at the earliest opportunity of the status of treaties and other agreements between indigenous peoples and States, as well as treaties between indigenous peoples and States, as well as treaties between States affecting indigenous peoples.

* The United Nations General Assembly should respond to the recommendations of indigenous and other organizations over the past decade, as well as that of the United Nations Sub-Commission's Special Rapporteur, and proclaim 1992 to be the 'International Year of the World's Indigenous Peoples'.

The Disappeared*

"Wherever law ends, tyranny begins."

John Locke, 1690

Disappearances, a sinister form of political repression, were first documented systematically in the mid-1970s by the Latin American media and human rights organizations. Since then, greater awareness of the widespread use of clandestine abductions and torture to terrorize and silence opponents has helped expose the various regimes which attempt to cloak their abuse of human rights in secrecy and anonymity. Disappearances carried out by, or on behalf of, official authorities are now a recorded practice in some 35 countries around the world.

The clandestine nature of the practice, and the official silence and denials which condone and perpetuate it, go a long way to explain its methods and rationale. Disappearances are designed to paralyse and destroy dissent – invariably described as subversive – while maintaining a façade of the rule of law or semblance of democracy. They are prevalent in systems where an ideology of national security predominates and stability is defined in terms of maintaining the military and economic

---

* ICIHI Sectoral Report: *Disappeared: Technique of Terror*, Zed Books London/New Jersey 1986; Lokayan, Delhi 1987. Other language editions: French and Russian. Also to be published: Arabic, Indonesian, Japanese and Spanish.

supremacy of those in power. This entails the subordination of the interests of the individual to those of the State and is generally the context within which disappearances occur.

Disappearances are invariably associated with authoritarian regimes. In a free and open society where individual rights and freedoms and diverse opinions are respected, it would obviously be difficult to carry them out. However, not all oppressive regimes use disappearances as a means of coercion. Those, impervious to international opinion and confident of retaining their hold on power, rely more on overt forms of repression to suppress dissent.

Paramilitary groups with no defined legal status or official link with the government authorities, are used in order to carry out disappearances. Such groups facilitate the government's denial of all knowledge and responsibility and allow it to blame extremists beyond its control.

Snatch squads are allowed to act with impunity, spreading fear and terror throughout a community. The disavowal of any connection with these groups is often a key element in a repressive government's strategy to bolster its democratic appearance in the hope of avoiding international condemnation and the possibility of sanctions.

There is, as yet, no universal legal definition of disappearances, but its characteristics are easily distinguished from other situations where individuals are described as missing. A distinctive and determining factor in identifying a situation as a disappearance case is the deliberate intention of the authorities to abduct an individual using military, political or secret service officials, or by the intervention of groups acting with their explicit or implicit approval, for the purpose of intimidation or repression. Persistently denying their involvement, and thus the legal rights and existence of the individual, authorities insist they are unable to provide information on the whereabouts or fate of the abducted person. Disappearances are thus intrinsically different from other human rights abuses, such as extra-judicial killings, detention without trial, internment and torture while in custody.

Governments do not like being questioned about their human rights standards or being characterized as a repressive regime. They are prone to take advantage of the political turmoil which tends to prevail in situations in which disappearances occur to mask their own responsibility. This is often done through the use of a state of emergency which enables governments to resort to the use of discretionary powers or legislation by decree. They are thus in a position to flout the standard legal procedures universally recognized as essential to the protection of the individual against the abuse of power. Although a state of emergency, subject to certain conditions, is recognized under international law, all too frequently it is used as a pretext to eliminate political opponents and to disguise gross violations of human rights.

Whatever the circumstances or rationale used for the introduction of a state of emergency, as stipulated under the International Convenant on Civil and Political Rights, there is no situation that can justify contempt for fundamental human rights. These include the right to life, right to recognition as a person before the law, right to a fair trial, right to humane conditions of detention including the right not to be subjected to torture or to cruel, inhuman treatment or punishment.

The principal form of recourse in a country governed by the principles of law is through the court system and the application of *habeas corpus* or similar procedures. In Latin America it is known as *amparo* which literally means protection, the object being to ensure an enquiry into the lawfulness of an individual's detention. Even if no overt limitations are placed on such procedures, they cannot be effective in the absence of an independent judiciary.

Disappearances rarely occur in isolation. Other means of repression including press censorship compound the difficulty of highlighting these atrocities. Under authoritarian regimes, a free and vigorous press is, by definition, not possible. Even if not completely silenced, it can only operate by careful self-censorship or by risking reprisals. Journalists who have dared to investigate abductions are themselves often victims of the same fate.

Likewise, human rights activists or anyone who expresses concern over the fate of the disappeared are equally at risk of being harassed or abducted. Threats to family members, the fear of compromising individuals not associated with human rights agencies or other such groups, and the inherent difficulties of operating under a repressive regime, severely limit the work of organizations trying to assist the relatives of the disappeared and bring to light such atrocities.

It is thus difficult to estimate the extent of such practices. Actual cases which are known and documented may thus be just the tip of the iceberg. Owing to a climate of fear and intimidation, many countries lack any type of reporting mechanism. Organizations which do manage to collect data readily acknowledge that their figures are merely a fraction of the total number abducted. The suffering of the 'living dead', repugnant to any civilized society and an affront to our shared humanity, has prompted various organizations at the international, regional and local level to develop standards and mechanisms designed to facilitate the exposure of this abuse of human rights.

In 1980, in response to growing public concern about disappearances, the United Nations Commission on Human Rights established a Working Group on Enforced or Involuntary Disappearances. Notwithstanding the inherent constraints, including the limited resources, under which it operates, the Working Group has been instrumental in bringing pressure to bear on governments implicated in disappearances. It reports annually to the Commission on Human Rights but only on cases which are well substantiated. Since the Working Group is not in a position to make independent investigations, in the sense of going to a country and conducting its own enquiry, it relies mostly on local groups to provide the relevant documentation. The Working Group, for example, reported on 3,367 cases of disappearances carried out in Argentina under the previous regime. An official enquiry undertaken by the new government put the figure at 8,960 and press estimates, which many consider a more accurate reflection, range from 15,000 to 30,000.

The Working Group deals directly with governments. Its mandate is thus unique in that it is at the immediate disposal of families and can take rapid action to save human lives. However, the impact and scope of the Group's work is limited since it is largely reliant on local groups and individuals to provide the necessary information. Moreover, it depends on governments to make appropriate investigations and report

131

back on the whereabouts of the disappeared. Not too surprisingly, there is a huge discrepancy between the number of cases transmitted to governments and those which are resolved. In addition, unsatisfactory and contradictory responses from governments involve time-consuming clarification of facts which severely impedes the work of the Group.

Another body which looks into disappearances is the Human Rights Committee established in 1976 under the International Covenant on Civil and Political Rights. Eighty-five States have so far ratified it but only thirty-eight are parties to its Optional Protocol which grants the Committee the right to consider communications from individuals and non-governmental organizations. The Committee reports annually on its deliberations to the United Nations General Assembly. This is its only means of sanction against a State which fails to fulfil its obligations.

The International Labour Organization (ILO) has adopted numerous Conventions relating to human rights such as freedom of association, protection from forced labour, and non-discrimination. In common with all such international organizations, it does not have the power to impose compliance but it has developed various mechanisms to monitor the application of standards. In connection with the disappearance of a trade union leader, for example, the Committee on Freedom of Association considers complaints received from unions, employer's organizations, and governments. If the government fails to respond satisfactorily, the ILO Director-General may approach it directly for additional information or, as in the case of Argentina in 1978, may send a representative to the country in question. This can sometimes put pressure on the government to obtain its co-operation.

The United Nations Educational, Scientific and Cultural Organization (UNESCO), concerned with the rights to freedom of thought and expression, has developed a number of procedures to deal with disappearances. Complaints may be filed by individuals, associations or international organizations when substantiated with reliable information. The Committee of Conventions and Recommendations of UNESCO may, during the course of its meetings which are held in the presence of representatives of the governments concerned, invite witnesses or those who have filed complaints to give testimony. The Committee may publicize evidence of human rights abuses in its Report or submit cases to the General Conference of UNESCO. However, the work of the Committee is not well known since it receives only a few cases annually.

Regional inter-governmental organizations such as the Council of Europe, the Organization of American States (OAS), the League of Arab Sates and the Organization of African Unity (OAU) have developed or are in the process of developing procedures complementary to the mechanisms which operate at the international level. These range from the European Court of Human Rights, in which cases on behalf of individuals can be heard and reparations awarded if the accused party, the State, is found guilty, to the Inter-American Commission on Human Rights which sends investigatory missions, prepares reports on countries, and considers complaints filed by individuals. The European Commission on Human Rights, which is empowered to consider complaints by individuals covered by the European Convention, has investigated disappearances within its area of competence. On the other hand, the absence or inadequacy of regional human rights mechanisms for countries in Africa, Asia and Eastern Europe continues to be a matter of great concern.

In sum, progress has been made in recent years to codify international law in respect of human rights but much remains to be done in strengthening what are, in effect, very fragile procedures to protect individuals against the abuse of power.

It is, perhaps, not too surprising, given the reality of relations between States and the many factors which determine how they interact, that the inter-governmental organizations they establish generally tend to be cautious and slow. However, non-governmental organizations (NGOs), sometimes described as the 'oxygen' essential to international human rights bodies, are often instrumental in generating public awareness of disappearances by making information available and bringing pressure to bear on inter-governmental organizations to take appropriate action.

NGOs have the advantage of flexibility which allows them to adapt to the circumstances of different situations. Quite often they are the best equipped to undertake in-depth studies on the

133

methods used in disappearances and compile information which is frequently necessary to expose the apparatus of a repressive regime. They also provide moral and material support to those whose rights have been denied. Their independence allows them to publicize their investigations, increase public awareness and mobilize international action. National groups are often in a unique position to act as an 'early warning system' by alerting the international community to the first signs of political repression.

In the course of our discussions in the Commission, we reviewed the role of the NGOs active in the field. They are too numerous to mention here. Their methods of work have been commented upon in the ICIHI Sectoral Report on the subject. We believe that the public and governments need to strengthen their support for the NGOs active in this hazardous and challenging area.

The ability of the international community to put an end to the odious practice of disappearances is hampered by the very nature of the phenomenon. Unlike other types of repression which are visible, disappearances are cloaked in anonymity, which compounds the difficulty of tracing those responsible and bringing the evidence to light. The application of *habeas corpus* or *amparo* provides concrete means of recourse and is thus an essential prerequisite for abolishing disappearances. A major question, therefore, is how can respect for, and effectiveness of the legal apparatus, be strengthened?

Many organizations have called for a new convention. However, its potential usefulness has been questioned since disappearances are already forbidden under existing international law. This is a valid argument. Nonetheless, even though the existence of a law does not automatically guarantee freedom from human rights violations, any measures at the international level to increase individual protection and the effectiveness of verification procedures necessary for obtaining evidence and imposing sanctions, would be a step in the right direction.

Since the initiation of a state of emergency is often the forerunner of human rights abuses, States should be urged to ensure that no violations occur while such measures are taken.

It has also been proposed that, as a way of preventing

disappearances from occurring while persons are held in prison, a bound registration book with numbered pages be maintained in each place of detention recording the identity of each individual, the reasons for imprisonment, the authority which took this decision, and the exact date of imprisonment, release or transfer to another institution.

The effectiveness of procedures currently available to international bodies and their ability to ensure a more rapid response to disappearance cases would be enhanced if they were empowered to utilize means of 'direct contact' with the governments concerned, and if the relevant bodies were ready to intervene at all times and not just during periodic working sessions. Effectiveness would also be increased if urgent cases were given priority and if there was the possibility of intervening before all internal recourses have been exhausted.

When it is not possible, owing to the conditions in which people are abducted, to obtain undeniable proof of the involvement of the authorities in disappearances, consideration could be given to circumstantial evidence. Full account should be taken of the behaviour patterns of the States concerned.

The Organization of American States and the Council of Europe have both condemned disappearances as a crime against humanity. However, the concept and the supporting legal structures are, as yet, extremely vague. If penal law at the international level is to be effective, then appropriate structures must be developed to ensure its application.

The most effective sanction by international organizations, in the sense of penalty or punishment, is publication of their findings and condemnation of abuses. Publicity, therefore, should be used to greater effect to highlight and combat disappearances. For example, a scale of publicity ranging from confidential investigations to open debates identifying the authorities and individuals concerned could be adopted.

Time and again it has been proved that loud and widespread condemnation is one of the most effective and feared weapons which can be employed against the perpetrators of human rights violations. This is particularly true in relation to disappearances, clouded as they always are in secrecy. Relatives' associations and human rights organizations which bear the brunt of the burden in exposing these practices deserve the strongest support possible. Solidarity is essential, as is financial and technical assistance, since the organizations are often hampered by lack of resources.

Public opinion has played a crucial role in making human rights a more prominent issue and is becoming increasingly important in international relations and influencing State behaviour. It is vital, therefore, that the public is constantly on the alert and does not become immune to the sickening repetition of oppression and the pain and horror that goes with it. Our collective determination to eradicate violations of human rights, such as disappearances, is the only way of ending them.

At the national level, we call upon governments:

* To respect fundamental human rights even during a state of emergency. In particular, they must immediately inform people and other States of the grounds for such action, the nature of the measures taken, and the specific rights which are suspended. International bodies should have at their disposal the means to make known the cases where such notification is not given.

* To give greater weight to circumstantial evidence in the case of disappearances where irrefutable proof cannot be obtained through legal investigations or eye-witness reports. Such evidence should take into account the behaviour pattern of the State concerned and should have consequences comparable to those of objective proof. Thus the authorities should be taken to task whenever it is established that:

  – they have shirked their obligations over a given period of time;
  – there is a manifest discrepancy between the facts of the case and public statements;
  – there is proof of insufficient diligence in the search for disappeared persons.

* To consider circumstantial evidence applicable in cases where the authorities failed to keep a regularly updated register of detainees in all places of detention.

At the international level, we are of the opinion that:

* International bodies, in their present or future work methods,

should adopt simple and speedy procedures designed to match the urgent nature of the problem. These should include, to the extent possible:

- direct contact with the parties concerned;
- the designation of bodies empowered to act between formal sessions;
- the possibility for some cases to be given priority on the agenda;
- the option to intervene even before all national remedies have been exhausted.

⋆ It would also be desirable for the United Nations Working Group on Enforced or Involuntary Disappearances to have a mandate of longer duration.

⋆ There should be, at all times, available as public documents, an up-to-date list of countries which declare or rescind a state of emergency. Within the United Nations, such a list could be the responsibility of the Sub-Commission on the Prevention of Discrimination and the Protection of Minorities.

⋆ Just as there are graduated punishments in penal law, so a graduated scale of public exposure could be developed and implemented by international organizations. The degree of exposure or publicity given would depend on the strength of proof obtained against the authorities concerned, on the gravity of their actions (isolated cases or routine practice), and on their willingness to co-operate.

We are furthermore of the opinion that:

⋆ Individuals involved in disappearances should be held responsible, on a personal basis, for crimes attributable to them. They should then be subject to the corresponding punishment as opposed to collective responsibility and sanctions.

⋆ Although many think that the practice of disappearances should be considered a crime against humanity, the concept is laden with historical connotations. It does not take into account certain elementary principles rooted in statutory and common law, such as prescription and non-retroactivity. We feel that a more appropriate concept would be to qualify the practice as *lèse-humanité*, or offence against humanity, which should be developed with the necessary provisions for its application.

* Information must be made to circulate even more widely, through the written word, in books and articles, as well as through the media and public meetings. The press, with all the resources at its disposal, must draw the attention of the public at large to the hidden drama of disappearances.

6. Man-Made Disasters

"Burn down your cities and leave our farms, and your cities will spring up again as if by magic; but destroy our farms and the grasses will grow in the streets of every city in the country."

William Jennings Bryan, 1826

Our Commission came together not only to better identify and understand some of the great humanitarian issues of our time, but also to press for action. In addition to examining past and present practices affecting human welfare, we also felt that we should look forward and try to anticipate the humanitarian issues of the future. Our work on man-made disasters is, thus, an attempt to understand problems of the future by looking at present-day policies.

We were particularly concerned to understand the causes of the famine in Africa and the ways in which future tragedies of this kind might be averted or diminished. We believe that humanitarianism does not mean simply giving temporary relief to human-beings in distress. It also involves seeking with them ways to improve their future, which means, on the one hand, recognizing the value of the human-being and, on the other, making human solidarity a central concept in reducing internal and external inequalities.

In addition to the processes of desertification and deforestation which are affecting tens of millions of people, we also examined new man-made disasters. Tragedies, such as those of Bophal and Chernobyl, are warnings to us all that industrial and nuclear accidents can have widespread effects. We believe that early warning systems, better preparedness and disaster management are important humanitarian goals. Human folly can cause suffering; but a better understanding of root causes can help us mitigate if not avoid it. We firmly believe that it is not enough to analyse contemporary problems facing human-kind exclusively from scientific, economic or political viewpoints. The humanitarian aspect, which is often neglected in the policy-making process, must be brought to the forefront. It is with this objective in mind that we reviewed problems such as deforestation and desertification as we examined contemporary food crises.

Contemporary Food Crises

When we began our work on humanitarian issues, a serious food crisis was endangering the lives of millions of human-beings in Africa. That is why we devoted our efforts in the first place to identifying the causes of that dramatic situation and the ways and means to prevent its recurrence. Following a Sectoral Report[1] relating to famine, published in 1985, which emphasized the threat of environmental degradation and the decisive role played by humans in bringing about the disaster upon themselves, two further studies were prepared and published on desertification[2] and deforestation.[3] Their scope goes beyond Africa since both desertification and deforestation are global issues affecting the well-being of present and future generations.

Many of the conclusions and recommendations we made in the context of the African famine, particularly those concerning aid policies, the organization of development aid, the role of non-governmental organizations and the range of national economic and social policy options, are also relevant to Asia and Latin America.

---

1. ICIHI Sectoral Report: *Famine: A Man-Made Disaster?*, Pan Books, London/Sydney, 1985. Also published in English by Random House, New York. Other language editions: Arabic, French, Italian, Japanese, Portuguese, Serbo-Croatian and Spanish. Also to be published in Bulgarian, Russian and Urdu.
2. ICIHI Sectoral Report: *The Encroaching Desert: The Consequences of Human Failure*, Zed Books, London/New Jersey, 1986. Also published in English by College Press, Zimbabwe, 1986; Arena Press, Hong Kong, 1987 and Lokayan Publishers, India, 1987. Other language editions: Arabic, Chinese and French. Also to be published in Russian and Spanish.
3. ICIHI Sectoral Report: *The Vanishing Forest: The Human Consequences of Deforestation*, Zed Books, London/New Jersey, 1986. Also published in English by College Press, Zimbabwe, 1986; Arena Press, Hong Kong, 1987;

Famine

During the 1980s, food crises occurred in the context of worsening terms of trade between developing and developed countries, an increasing external debt which was becoming unmanageable, growing domestic inequality and, in many cases, rapidly expanding populations. These factors, each at its own specific pace, combined to make national economies, particularly those in Africa, acutely vulnerable. The drought of 1984–85, which affected vast regions of Africa, exposed the structural weaknesses which exist in many developing countries on that continent and elsewhere.

In Africa more than anywhere else, the lack of a sufficiently credible early warning system, of dynamic innovation in inter-state relations, and of adequately co-ordinated relief mechanisms, were factors which delayed the deployment of international aid. For millions of rural dwellers, aid came too late. Many had already died or were starving and those who had lost their livelihood were flocking to the cities in search of elusive odd jobs or crossing national borders to face an uncertain future in the refugee camps.

Food aid did, of course, enable many to survive, but it failed to replace the means of production lost during the crisis. Many farmers, for example, were unable to take advantage of the late 1985 rains because they had no seeds, no animals, and no money. To be realistic, one must recognize that for years to come the crisis caused by drought and famine will have the gravest consequences for the most vulnerable social groups and for African economies as a whole.

If the rainfall remains adequate in the coming years, it would relieve the economic situation to a certain extent. But it will take a long time for Africa to overcome the economic losses of recent years. People will not simply flock back to the farms. It will take a long time to repair the broken social fabric and even longer to roll back the desert or regenerate the forest. The

Lokayan Publishers, India, 1987 and Sun Books, Malaysia, 1987. Other language editions: Chinese, French, Russian and Serbo-Croatian. Also to be published in Indonesian, Japanese, Spanish and Thai.

consequences of good and bad years are not symmetrical. The structural problems still have to be faced, however good the rains for a time may be.

For a better assessment of the role played by climatic factors, it is not enough to go back a few years in time. Only decades or centuries can give a true perspective. History shows that there is nothing exceptional about the recent droughts. Six similar periods have been identified in the Sahel since the beginning of the 15th century, each lasting some 10 to 20 years. The period from 1790 to 1850 was particularly dry and another starting in 1895 culminated in the dramatic years 1911 to 1914. From the 1931 famine in Niger until 1950, Sahel countries suffered a number of droughts.

During these dry years, the mandatory development of cash crops, such as cotton and groundnuts, at the behest of the colonial administrations, adversely affected the fertility of the fragile soil. In 1936–37, the Franco-British Forestry Commission reported that the Sahara was on the move and called on the authorities to stop deforestation. The warning went unheeded.

In retrospect, the 1950s and early 1960s in Sub-Saharan Africa look like very favourable years. They had, in fact, the highest rainfall since the turn of the century. During the 1950s the rainfall was above average in the Sudan zone, by 10 to 20 per cent, by 20 to 30 per cent in the Sahelian zone and by 50 to 60 per cent in the Sahelian–Saharan zone. The rain made it possible to extend cultivation northwards, particularly in the Sahel. More cash crops were produced without any apparent loss of food production. In this context, these points should be made:

Firstly, unlike any other part of the world, Africa displays remarkable spatial coherence in its climate patterns. Rainfall tends to be favourable or unfavourable all over the continent during the same periods. There can, of course, be relative variations. These tend to be greater in East than in West Africa.

Secondly, an important part of African rainfall comes from local evaporation, the rest being linked to the general circulation of atmospheric currents. Any dry year therefore means less evaporation and even less precipitation the following year, until the sequence is broken by a compensating mechanism which is one of nature's secrets, not yet fully comprehensible to the experts. Meteorology is still unable to predict when this compensating mechanism comes into play. Nor can it be said that the climate has changed: a number of different assumptions have been made, none of which has been unanimously accepted by the world scientific community.

Thirdly, governments and planners quite wrongly consider a bad year unusual. But a normal climate is made up of good and bad years and an alternating pattern between them is quite common.

The rainfall records for West Africa show that in the mid-1960s an irregular but persistent drier trend appeared. The 1972–73 drought in the Sahel, East Africa and Ethiopia and the events associated with it – famine, population movements, refugees etc. – highlighted the importance of climatic variability.

African governments, experts, and public opinion in the donor countries suddenly became aware of something farmers all over the world have always known: a normal climate has its ups and downs. But, of course, a drought in arid and semi-arid areas can cause famine when not enough food has been put aside, or when local prices fluctuate and not enough money is available to purchase what food is available.

The importance given suddenly to climatic variability was all the greater as the drought and food shortage in 1972–73 not only affected Africa, but also Asia and Latin America. This combination of factors gave the crisis a world dimension which was highlighted at the 1974 World Food Conference.

Many analysts tried to link the crisis to a single cause and two clearly distinct views prevailed. Supporters of the status quo blamed the weather while advocates of change blamed social and political structures.

Gradually, between these two extremities of theory, new studies began to stress the inter-relations between climatic, social, economic and political factors. Because it was so difficult to take all these factors into account, governments and experts came to treat the people who had been living in the intricate web of causative factors for centuries, namely the farmers, with a little more respect. The strategies they had devised over time to ensure survival in an uncertain and often hostile environment, were no longer systematically denigrated.

While planners still regarded bad years as unusual, early warning systems began to be developed to forecast potential bad harvests by monitoring rainfall data and the growth of crops. At the same time, research showed that cultivators and herders had their own warning systems.

The renewed droughts of 1984–85 were the final blow for the development theories of the 1950s. Both African governments and donor countries now accept the need for adequate preparedness and the setting up of early warning systems based on weather data, crop monitoring as well as social and economic indicators. At the same time, detailed studies of traditional crops and livestock farming methods have been initiated in order to make them less vulnerable to climatic fluctuations.

These are small but important steps forward, but measures like them tend to be set aside when things improve. The pressure to revert to old habits remains strong. It is important, therefore, to remember that early warning systems are not simply a set of technological measures based on the vagaries of climate and agriculture. They also recognize something that has been forgotten for too long: the most humble cultivator or herder has a wealth of experience and resourcefulness.

Since our first plenary meetings in 1984, devoted largely to the food crises, we are pleased to note that many of our views and suggestions are increasingly reflected in national and international policies. Clearly, occasional food shortages in developing countries cannot be eliminated but famine situations can certainly be averted through foresight and timely action. For this purpose, we feel that there is continued need to develop and adopt efficient and reliable early warning systems. It is not enough to depend on the present national estimates, often based on unreliable assumptions about population size, national crop area and the likely yields. Famine forecasting should take into account human behaviour as much as crop behaviour. We recommend in this connection a monitoring system, particularly in the known vulnerable areas, based on a series of agreed indicators concerning the fluctuations of local market food prices and other warning signs, such as farmers selling livestock and household goods or migrating to other areas.

Satellite photography is beginning to play an increasingly important role in identifying areas where crop failures are likely to occur. Such technological advances must be coupled with socio-economic research at the local level. In other words, satellite engineers and meteorologists must join forces with agronomists and social scientists.

More often than not, food policies are made by urban people for urban people. Those living in rural areas, invariably the majority in the developing countries, have no voice and no role to play. In this context, the price structure and agriculture production policies become the decisive factors in precipitating, or averting, national food emergencies. We are firmly of the opinion that the needs and aspirations of farmers must have a decisive role in the planning of agricultural policies now elaborated by urban experts. There must be a concerted policy of turning the urban–rural terms of trade away from the cities in favour of the countryside by ensuring that small farmers in developing countries receive adequate returns for their products.

At the same time, while we are convinced that food aid should be provided generously to those in need, it is equally important that such aid be carefully controlled and managed. Food aid should be made available for a pre-determined and finite period of time in order to avoid undue dependency. In known vulnerable areas, local food storage depots should be established and special attention should be paid to problems of logistics, delivery and distribution.

Governments and banks should develop schemes to provide credit facilities directly to small-scale farmers so that they can get through difficult periods without feeling obliged to abandon their lands and move elsewhere. Donors would do well to offer collateral to local banks instead of providing straight hand-outs to governments so that financial support is provided, on a self-help basis, to farmers directly. At the same time, it is vital to reduce the debt burden of afflicted governments and allow them the time to recover. It would also be helpful if there were a more generous transfer of technology and a sharing of research, particularly on genetic engineering and agro-forestry, and assistance with the establishment of local gene banks.

The food crisis in Africa should sharpen our sense of common humanity. The problems faced by Africans are not theirs alone – whether in their making, their implications or the solutions that must be found for them. They are problems which Africans, like suffering people in other developing regions, share with the rest of the world. Global co-operation is thus not peripheral but central to the survival of millions of human-beings.

This is all the more so since, alongside the crisis of penury in the Third World, there is also a crisis of abundance in the First World. At the same time as hundreds of millions of our fellow human-beings suffer from malnutrition, or die of starvation, there is a glut of 400 million tons of surplus grain generated by Western Europe and North America. It is a crisis because government subsidies to farmers in the West amounting to billions of dollars and keeping the prices artificially high for the consumers are now becoming a serious economic, social and political problem. The European Community is reported to be considering destroying 20 million metric tons of beef, butter and grain because their storage alone costs some $4 billion. Last year, the United States was reported to have spent $6 billion on subsidizing the export of corn worth $2 billion.

This crisis of abundance is not going to subside. The spectacular advances in genetic engineering are going to help enhance the capacity to produce much more with much less effort. Commonsense calls for a global plan for food security which is based on a precise determination of world production levels coupled with levels of production for each country and region. But this requires a political climate at global level based on mutuality and human solidarity which at present is lamentably lacking.

Basic food requirements must not be allowed to fall prey to power politics. There is greater awareness of this among people than among governments. We are encouraged, however, by recent developments which show an increased sensitivity on the part of policy-makers to the importance of agriculture – a domain that has for decades been way down on the list of national priorities. The recently initiated Uruguay Round, which will lead to agricultural policies being negotiated in the context of the General Agreement on Tariffs and Trade

(GATT), is a step in the right direction. Adjusting prices and production systems, sharing the benefits of technological advances, promoting self-sufficiency among the poor nations are measures called for not merely by economic or political considerations. In our view, they are essentially humanitarian issues which demand the urgent attention of policy-makers.

Desertification

"Our land, compared with what it was, is like the skeleton of a body wasted by disease."

Plato, 360 B.C.

The great deserts like the Sahara and the Kalahari in Africa, the Atacama in South America, the Rajasthan desert in South Asia, and many others, are all growing. The term 'desertification' does not, however, refer only to the forward surge of the desert. It can also refer to the loss of the land's viability due to soil erosion and reduction of vegetative cover and organic matter. These factors can affect all climatic zones, even humid, tropical and temperate ones.

In arid and semi-arid areas, the rapid loss of biological potential has dramatic consequences for the poor who live there. Desertification is accelerated by excessive livestock numbers which lead to overgrazing, by intensive farming in high climatic risk areas, and by the felling – without replanting – of trees for firewood or timber. Many proposals have been put forward to reduce livestock numbers. Most of them, however, do not take sufficiently into account the great variety of social, cultural, technological and economic factors and inter-relationships which stimulate the growth of herds.

To reduce the consumption of firewood, fuel-efficient stoves were suggested. They are gradually being introduced but government officials often tend to neglect this type of effort. It is easier to plant 10,000 eucalyptus trees than to get families to switch to more effective stoves. Most governments are more receptive to the modern appearance of a carefully laid out plantation, than to the need for stoves, however efficient they might be. Moreover a plantation, like a road, a new building or

147

a dam, can be officially inaugurated, and there is much political capital to be made. But sometimes tree plantations can actually accelerate desertification by draining groundwater. In the best of cases, the plantation will yield only one product such as firewood, timber or pulp, and only a handful of by-products. It cannot be compared to a natural forest made up of different types of trees of all ages, serving all kinds of purposes.

Reducing the size of herds, lowering the consumption of firewood by fuel-efficient stoves and by substitution with other sources of energy, planting new forests with a variety of trees after consulting the local rural population, are some of the steps to combat desertification in arid areas.

Another general method is often mentioned – irrigation. One very important feature in all arid areas is the irregular rainfall. The drier the climate, the greater the difference between rainy and dry years, and consequently the more vulnerable the crops and livestock. Therefore building dams and large-scale irrigation schemes would seem a logical answer to drought and desertification.

Unfortunately, ambitious irrigation systems can also be among the causes of desertification because salt accumulates in the surface layers when irrigation is not combined with appropriate drainage. The irrigation of saline soil has been the scourge of many civilizations since time immemorial. But governments and the officials of financial institutions ignore the lessons of the past when embarking on grand, large-scale irrigation projects.

From the initial political, technical and financial decisions to the actual irrigation of the first plots of land, five to ten years may elapse. During the first few years of operation, many new factors come into play and may prevent a clear assessment of the project. By the time it is realized that something serious has gone wrong, fifteen or twenty years have gone by. That is much longer than any ordinary government's political time frame. When serious difficulties do emerge, experts are sent to conduct a survey among the farmers who are held to be primarily responsible. Indeed, who else could be blamed for the failure? Certainly not the infallible experts!

Large-scale irrigation schemes are often presented as the most appropriate answer to the grave problems of arid and semi-arid countries. But in fact the planning, implementation and operation of those schemes too often take place without reference to the recipient communities who are treated as passive users unable to reason or speak for themselves.

There is, therefore, a tendency among decision-makers in planning agencies, banks and government departments to disregard human diversity and the wealth of experience it represents. Obscured by cost-benefit analyses which reflect their own criteria and values, they regard the end-users as economic objects moulded in their own image. Yet these cultivators and herders are the everyday users who make or break a project.

The greater the area covered by a given project, the more complex and time-consuming the process of consultation becomes. Initially those in charge may be sincerely intent on consultation, but material and time constraints soon gain the upper hand. Large-scale projects still follow the same pattern: as soon as financing possibilities appear, the project must be formulated quickly so as not to let the opportunity slip by. When financing has been agreed upon, credit agencies (for financial reasons) and governments (for political reasons) start pushing to get the job done. There is not enough time for a detailed study of the environmental, societal and cultural complexities in which those primarily concerned would take part.

Declarations favouring community involvement are made, but effective participation does not fit in with the time constraints of bankers, politicians and managers. Irrigation schemes do not fail because they are too large. They fail because they are not supervised on a day-to-day basis and do not take into account the implications for the users. They fail also because they disregard the essential element of human solidarity. For there can be no sharing of water resources over space and time without a solidarity best expressed by groupings which institutionalize sharing as well as the settling of disputes.

It has often been observed that many deep wells drilled by government agencies to mitigate the effects of drought and desertification have actually led to overgrazing and accelerated desertification in the surrounding areas. This has occurred especially when the wells have not been specifically allocated to communities which could have regulated their use on a customary basis. Even small-scale water projects are subject to administrative regulations imposed without consulting the users. The same is true of many measures taken to combat desertification, such as tree planting and dune consolidation.

This kind of government attitude is particularly regrettable in the case of pastoral areas and nomadic herders for two different humanitarian reasons. Firstly, because governments do not take into account the knowledge of people who have managed for centuries the highly complex activity of nomadic livestock-raising. Secondly, because herders, both individually and collectively, suffer the most during droughts.

Merely to help herders survive is a gesture which is both ethically incomplete and practically ineffective in the long run if there is no active recognition of, and respect for, their know-how and social and cultural values. That recognition is essential if they are to adapt to new economic, social, technological and cultural conditions without being deprived of their integrity and identity. Facing up to the new challenges must not involve resisting all change any more than destroying past values and customs. Between the museum and the shanty town, there is a place for a kind of change ensuring mutual respect for the different customs of others, something nomadic societies have practised for centuries.

Nomadic pastoralism is a well-tried and successful use of arid land. Imbalances causing a loss of fertility are brought about by externally induced changes: changes in herd structure geared to demand from cities and richer countries for cattle rather than the traditional camel which is better suited to local conditions; changes in the behaviour of settled farmers using pastoral land to plant more crops and themselves raising livestock; changes also in livestock practices with the emergence of new absentee landlords (civil servants and businessmen from the city) who see no better investment alternatives.

New landlords, keen on quick financial returns, contribute greatly to overgrazing and environmental degradation. Those who tend their herds find themselves in a new situation where their employer's instructions or the government's regulations are no longer consonant with social custom. In this situation, the remedies for desertification may not be found on the rangelands but in the cities where different investment incentives beneficial to the national economy should be provided. Desertification, therefore, is not only a self-contained technical issue; it must be viewed in a wider perspective taking into account society and the economy as a whole.

The United Nations Conference on Desertification held in Nairobi in 1977 adopted a Plan for Action to Combat Desertification. In the Report we published on desertification,[1] we listed the errors of donors and recipients alike, analysed failures and successes, and stressed the lack of adequate financial resources and co-ordination. The recommendations made in the Report emphasize, in particular, community participation. Financial resources are insufficient and the co-ordination between national and international bodies is poor. But what the Plan really missed was a recognition of basic human needs, rights, dignity and creativeness, as well as a framework for analysis of the national economy and its relationship with the world economy.

We are of the opinion that taking into account all these factors, and in addition to the suggestions made earlier, desertification control must be organized around a completely different approach covering three main aspects:

* The revision of policies which accelerate desertification, in particular export-oriented farming, forestry and livestock activities.

* The mobilization of local human resources to ensure reorganization based on participation, and of agricultural, breeding and veterinary research, education and extension.

* More equitable sharing of resources between different social groups and nations.

---

1. *The Encroaching Desert*, op. cit.

Deforestation

"Trees are the earth's endless efforts to speak to the listening heavens."

Rabindranath Tagore, 1928.

The moist areas close to the Equator, far removed from the nearest desert, seem to run no risk of desertification. The forest belt around the Equator appears both powerful and fertile. But that picture is misleading. The higher the temperature, the quicker the degradation of organic matter. And organic matter is essential to maintain soil fertility. In colder climates, it accumulates on the ground in a thick layer which becomes a reservoir of fertility. Things are quite different near the Equator. With heavy and regular rainfall the year round, degradation is quick and continuous and the soil holds very little organic matter.

The most luxuriant forests are actually growing on the world's poorest soils. This is a paradox due to a long adaptation process which permits almost all the organic matter to be recycled in the thin humus layer at the surface. If the trees disappear, the soil is rapidly depleted of its humus by rainfall, a process known as leaching. The moist tropical forest soil is also rich in iron and aluminium. When the forest, or the secondary vegetation which replaces it, is destroyed and the land cultivated, exposure to the sun and rain turns the soil surface into brick-hard laterite. The harm done is practically irreversible. Using the term desertification to describe only arid and semi-arid areas, one tends to forget that the loss of biological potential is also considerable in tropical zones.

Tropical forests are being cleared for lumber and to make way for plantations, pastures and crops. The importance given to different uses varies from country to country and over time according to the relative weight of the various interests involved. States, big national and international investors, farmers looking for more land, or landless peasants eager to get their first plot constitute some of the external forces accelerating deforestation. But the forests are not empty: people have been occupying them for centuries and, with very few exceptions, they have to suffer the disastrous consequences of deforestation because they do not have the political, social or economic power to preserve their livelihood, their way of life and their culture.[1]

The theory that population pressure makes the gradual clearing of all forests inevitable must be carefully examined. Pressure is, of course, exerted by populations from outside the forest areas since the number of people living in or around the forests has barely increased at all, and in some cases has stagnated or decreased.

In some countries, landless peasant immigration into forest areas has been encouraged by the government. The landless and unemployed are given land, but after a few harvests the soil is depleted. The forests are also felled for wood. The main causes here are no longer population pressure but short-sighted policies resulting from governments' balance of payments problems. Trees are felled for economic gain or repaying the external debt.

Cutting down trees for firewood is not a major cause of destruction in moist tropical forests, but it is an important cause of deforestation in dry areas. Where there is an established wood and paper industry, for example, business interests may be responsible for long-term damage to mixed forests.

In tropical countries, massive woodland clearing is a recent phenomenon. The consequences are more serious than in temperate countries because the environment is more fragile and many more people live in and from the forest. However, because they are culturally, economically and politically marginalized, they are unable to make themselves heard and to fight for their rights. Moreover, in tropical and equatorial areas, traditional forest dwellers are vulnerable to the diseases brought in by newcomers, who in turn pick up other diseases in the tropical forest or newly cleared areas. Neither group has the time to build up its immunity system.

Deforestation also modifies the habitat of animals which are a reservoir of tropical forest diseases (monkeys and rodents in

---

1. ICIHI Sectoral Reports *The Vanishing Forest: The Human Consequences of Deforestation* and *Indigenous Peoples: A Global Quest for Justice*, 1987, op. cit.

particular), and of insects which communicate them to man (mosquitoes, flies, bugs, etc). The development of new human settlements without appropriate sanitation gives rise to other health problems such as the proliferation of intestinal parasites. The Sectoral Report we published on deforestation covers this often neglected field of the health consequences flowing from the clearing of tropical forests.

All large tropical forest areas shelter tribal groups. Often they are small groups of hunter–gatherers or shifting cultivators moving over large areas, adapting their life-style to the forest ecosystem, and ensuring their own subsistence without depleting forest resources. By adapting to forest conditions, these groups learned to control and cure endemic diseases in their own way. But any imported disease can have fatal consequences. Examples of this are to be found all over the world, but the most striking are probably in Brazil. There were six to nine million Amerindians there at the beginning of the 16th century. Today, barely 200,000 survive. The total number of tribes has dropped from 230 in 1900 to about half that number. Even ordinary and curable infections, such as measles or the common cold, can be fatal to tribal people, especially children.

The gradual clearing of forests has, of course, serious ecological consequences. Forests play an important part in regulating climate in general, and micro-climates and water flows in particular. On hills and slopes, when the trees are gone, there is nothing to prevent erosion and the loss of topsoil, and the land becomes useless. Rainwater, which cannot drain sufficiently, swells the rivers and floods are more frequent. The water carries away the finer particles of earth which silt up dams and make them less efficient. Rivers widen because their beds rise and floods cover a greater area.

With deforestation, thousands of animal and plant species also disappear. Most of them have never been studied and their biological and economic potential has, thus, disappeared forever. Valuable genetic resources built up over millions of years have been lost. Some of them were used by forest dwellers who had come to understand their healing power or food value. The destruction of traditional ways of life means that valuable knowledge has disappeared not only about forest products and their uses but also, in large measure, about the management of the fragile ecological forest balance.

It is possible to use the surviving forests without destroying them. An appropriate combination of agriculture and forestry, agroforestry as it is called, can both ensure a maximum use of forest resources and preserve them for future generations. Similarly, wild fauna can be managed more efficiently than imported livestock.

Agroforestry is practised all over the world. The forest management techniques of tribal peoples must be studied scientifically. They must be regarded not as museum pieces but as living proof of world diversity.

Such studies must involve action-oriented research with community participation. They should help forest dwellers to cope more effectively with a changing way of life. Putting humanitarian concerns first does not mean sacrificing economic considerations, but merely re-orienting them. Governments must try to reduce the pressure for forest clearing by changing agricultural policies (land reforms, other technological options, etc.) and by replacing destructive habits by sound resource management (gradual clearing, rotation, agroforestry, replanting, etc.).

We believe that humanitarian principles must play a central role in devising new solutions. Economists must be encouraged to take into account cultural and ecological diversity. They should recognize human creativity as well as the ethical and moral need for community involvement.

*   *   *

The overall review of contemporary food crises and the related problems of desertification and deforestation to which our Commission attached special importance have led us to the general conclusion that future policies and actions must take into account three fundamental considerations: *diversity, creativity, participation.* We noted with deep concern that, since the late 1950s and early 1960s, when many of them became politically independent, developing countries have suffered a consistent deterioration of their terms of trade. The prices of goods and services sold by industrial countries have risen or remained constant whereas the prices of commodities sold by developing countries have been stagnating or falling.

At the same time, bureaucracies in the newly independent States have expanded, sometimes beyond the limit which the economy could reasonably be expected to sustain. There certainly was a need for better education, health facilities and infrastructure, but the newly independent countries usually applied a Western-style model of development. The direct and indirect cost of that approach and its adverse effects on consumption patterns and life-styles are only now being recognized.

How can the best options be identified for sharing resources more equitably between rural and urban areas, improving food security for the most vulnerable groups and managing resources more carefully without depriving future generations of their rightful heritage? In order to choose the right options, a number of Third World leaders are now more inclined than ever before, to accept that there is an urgent need to draw up a checklist of all available technologies and organizational means. They also accept that experts alone are not enough and that all social and professional groups should be able to express their creativeness and put forward their own know-how, experience and perception. For instance, a systematic research programme should be undertaken with the main groups involved to analyse, and improve, agroforestry and nomadic livestock raising.

The development of scientific and technological thinking owes a lot to the practical knowledge accumulated by communities over centuries of observation and experience. After the first European scientific revolution, however, science distanced itself from folk sources. While there is no denying that scientific development since then has been spectacular, the classical scientist whose aim was to understand rather than dominate nature, actually dissociated himself from these traditions.

Scientists are now beginning to show more respect for approaches which borrow from Non-European traditions of agricultural, medicinal as well as livestock, water or forest management methods. They no longer ignore that knowledge but are scrutinizing it, disregarding what is wrong and keeping what could constitute more appropriate approaches for research and action in a given social and cultural environment.

These approaches will become more and more acceptable in developing countries in the future as the historically limited scope of science and technology becomes clearer. So far, scientific and technological development has followed the needs of industrialized countries. Some research sectors were not needed in those countries. For example, industrialized countries only became interested when the price of nitrogenous fertilizers rose – following the oil price surge – and it was only then that they began research on how bacteria could directly provide plants with nitrogen, a subject of considerable interest to Third World agriculture. Other research sectors specifically concerning conditions in tropical countries dealt with cash crops of interest to colonial powers instead of food crops. Today, many scientific and technological fields remain to be explored to satisfy the needs of tropical countries: scientific ecology and biotechnology have given rise to considerable hope.

The Sectoral Reports we published on famine, desertification and deforestation all call for an approach which takes environmental constraints into account in agricultural and rural development. Such developments must be sustainable in the long run, and at the same time provide the poorest with better access to food. It must ensure food security from season to season and from year to year.

Technological decisions must therefore be made to meet three needs: maintaining long-term renewability of essential natural resources; increasing agricultural production, in particular food production; and increasing self-sufficiency and purchasing power of the rural poor. Technological change must not push the rural poor towards cities which cannot absorb the influx either because the existing urban infrastructure is already stretched to the limit or because there are not enough employment opportunities.

Solidarity implies deep changes in relations between nations, between rural and urban areas, and between dominating and marginalized groups. Solidarity with future generations implies changes in the management of natural resources. There will be new famines and more violence and armed conflicts if such

157

changes do not start immediately to improve the lot of the poorest. These changes will have to follow new ethical rules governing the relationships between human societies and their environment, a new solidarity among human societies, and a new wisdom based on social as well as economic factors.

There is already a tendency to recognize the importance of cultural factors in development and the role of the so-called ecoculture combining cultural, social and environmental features. The way each group – forest dwellers, unemployed youth, nomadic herders – sees its own environment and makes the most of it can no longer be ignored in preparing aid and development policies and projects. Finally, the need for participation is gradually becoming more acceptable. The greater confidence being shown in these initiatives shows that the human-being is gradually coming to the fore, not only because of his suffering but also on account of his creative ability.

But favourable changes take time. New famines, armed conflicts and acts of violence are therefore to be expected and preparedness must be improved. Early warning systems are required to take timely action before a crisis occurs. While it is not easy to foresee armed conflicts and social violence, there is a well established sequence of events in famines which makes forecasting fairly reliable. Threatened groups have their own perception of such events. But they must be able to express themselves so that their views can be confronted with objective data. Early warning systems therefore require that cultivators and herders not be treated as objects. The systems must be credible enough for national and international solidarities to emerge before the outbreak of a food crisis, before panic sales of belongings, and before the population exodus begins.

Timely action also requires aid co-ordinating mechanisms. These can only be effective if relations between States and organizations are such as to give priority to humanitarian considerations. It is during the organization of aid distribution that government objections arise. We believe it inhuman to invoke the argument of national sovereignty to prevent relief supplies from reaching starving populations, even if they are hostile to the government. Hunger must not be allowed to become a weapon, like food aid. We note with concern that more often than not politics takes precedence over humanitarian concerns. The proposal to open 'mercy corridors' under international supervision, in order to give access to famine areas, must receive the support it deserves. But that is precisely the type of operation which can ensure the primacy of humanitarian concerns and the survival of millions of people.

In this context, it is worthwhile to recall the action of the United Nations Relief and Rehabilitation Organization (UNRRA) in China in 1945–47. A resolution by the UNRRA Council enabled it to distribute relief irrespective of who was controlling the territory. The resolution stated that at no time should relief and rehabilitation supplies be used as a political weapon, and no discrimination should be made in the distribution of relief supplies because of race, creed or political belief. That principle is as important today as it was then.

One of the practical problems with this approach is illustrated by the trials and tribulations of many development projects, including those of non-governmental organizations. NGOs, with their great diversity, can be divided into many categories, according to their local, national or international character, their sources of financing, their relations with national or international political forces. Where development projects use foreign volunteers – as they often do – the cultural gap is of course considerable, but it can be just as serious in the case of national officials belonging to another culture – city dwellers in rural areas for instance. When the authorities take the trouble to listen to rural populations and a true dialogue is established, projects are often successful. Many non-governmental organizations have learnt during the last 30 years to listen to the people they want to help. They have learnt that success is often dependent on respect for others and their different ways of life. Thus for practical reasons, the need for a mutually beneficial dialogue has emerged. That pragmatic realization itself has gradually given rise to an ethical assessment and to the recognition of universality through specificity. We believe that not only should that movement be supported, it should also be given a new impetus because successes have hitherto been local, partial and often temporary.

Factors explaining the micro-successes achieved by non-governmental organizations are often too specific to be extrapolated to a whole region or country. International project officials must remember that their own presence is relatively short-term, that their sacrifices are temporary and that they will have other jobs to go back to in their home countries when their enthusiasm wanes. But their counterparts in local administrations have nothing else to turn to. It is easy to accuse them of being incompetent, indifferent or corrupt, but this only exacerbates the latent antagonism between non-governmental and governmental organizations.

It should not be forgotten that the risks are of a different character and that failures do not have the same meaning. Non-governmental organizations can only play a pioneering role if their initiatives are copied, and in particular if they can provide new inspiration and motivation to governments and local authorities to ensure the general distribution of new ideas, methods or technology.

It is easier and more gratifying to recognize the human-being among the forest tribes, oppressed minorities, nomadic herders, poor farmers and shanty town dwellers than in local state officials and civil servants. A new effort is needed to expand the ethical framework to include the needs and human resourcefulness of all social actors who must endeavour to become partners, with rights and obligations, in their struggle for development. Instead of accusing and isolating the State, its representatives and bodies have to be enlightened and motivated to chart out this new direction.

New Man-Made Disasters*

"The certainties of one age are the problems of the next."

Richard H. Tawney, 1926

Hazards of Commercial Nuclear Power

Few subjects have generated more confusion and anxiety in recent years than the future of commercial nuclear power. A series of accidents in the nuclear industry have caused

---

* ICIHI Sectoral Report, *New Man-Made Disasters*, to be published in 1988.

widespread alarm and left governments searching for fresh ideas on how to handle nuclear energy. Never before have so many difficult questions been asked about the safety of nuclear technology for peaceful purposes and the ethics which underlie its use. This is why we paid special attention to this subject, particularly at our Stockholm meeting which took place at the time of the Chernobyl accident.

Nuclear power is championed as a politically and economically attractive means for producing energy. Many industrial States want to reduce their dependence on coal and avoid the fluctuating price of imported oil. Other States with scarce fossil-fuel resources feel that nuclear power represents the only realistic option for production of an abundant supply of energy. In Third World countries, where forests are threatened by the use of wood as a source of energy, nuclear power has been heralded as a reliable, inexhaustible and cost-effective alternative energy source.

Many believe that opting for commercial nuclear power is humane and that safe reactors are environmentally benign. It is argued that few people have lost their lives from the production of nuclear energy, as compared to the high number of workers injured or killed in coal mines. Furthermore, nuclear reactors do not produce acid rain which destroys forests and lakes and causes respiratory diseases for millions of people.

Yet despite its promise as a viable energy source, no one can deny that commercial nuclear power suffers from serious problems of technological and human error which must urgently be resolved. The consequences of these problems can cause death and misery across continents. All of the world's 374 commercial nuclear plants use uranium fuel which can melt down and spew out deadly radiation. Experts had predicted that the odds of a nuclear meltdown were one in 10,000 years. Now after Chernobyl and many other less widely reported accidents, many fear that nuclear disasters are a real, ever-present possibility.

The consequences of a major commercial nuclear accident are not amenable to precise quantification, but human and material costs could conceivably climb to intolerable levels. Those working at a nuclear plant, rescue workers and thousands of people in the immediate area are the most vulnerable to radiation exposure. In countries where nuclear plants are situated close to densely populated areas, the threat is of course proportionally greater. Furthermore, contamination from a nuclear accident can afflict wide regions causing cancer, genetic disorders and birth deformities for millions. This is due to the fact that radioactive clouds, like winds, respect no national borders.

Major nuclear accidents can jeopardize far more than physical health. Fertile land may be contaminated, forcing region-wide quarantines on crops and livestock. Decontaminating a damaged nuclear power station and the surrounding area can also entail colossal expenditures. Moreover, the emotional pressures of evacuating entire communities, of families getting displaced or scattered, and the inconvenience of constantly having to monitor the radiation levels of clothing, automobiles and buildings can become unbearable.

Accidents are not the only dangers posed by commercial nuclear power. Scientists have discovered how to produce energy from nuclear fuel, but have not yet found a globally adequate answer to the problem of high-level radioactive waste material produced by nuclear plants. The term waste disposal as used in reference to radioactive materials is really a misnomer because, owing to technological constraints and human fallibility, safe long-term disposal continues to evade a satisfactory solution.

Compounding the nuclear waste problem is the process of decommissioning over 300 commercial nuclear reactors that will wear out during the next three decades. A nuclear plant cannot simply be abandoned at the end of its useful life. Retired nuclear reactors must be dismantled and disposed of safely to protect the public from radioactivity. But before the decommissioning can proceed, all the high-level nuclear waste which was built up during its operating life must be removed from the plant and securely isolated from people and the environment.

No country is at present sufficiently prepared to handle the complex decommissioning process. The problem has been avoided because until now the need to dismantle major nuclear plants has not arisen. But time is running out for many old reactors. Radioactive materials remain highly toxic for centuries. They will be a lethal legacy for future generations.

Few modern technologies are without some potential risk to human life and the environment. The prosperity of the last two centuries is a result of scientific innovations despite the heavy price which their side-effects exacted and which governments accepted to pay. Thus, the unresolved problems of the nuclear industry do not necessarily lead to the conclusion that commercial nuclear power be abandoned. Aside from ethical reflections, a plea for terminating nuclear power is not practical. However, given the extent of its potential harm, it is imperative to weigh seriously humanitarian considerations for safeguarding its use and determining its future.

International Safeguards: We believe that governments have been hesitant in recognizing the magnitude of global risks posed by the nuclear industry and the need for internationally respected safeguards. Safety concerns continue to be guided by national standards while the consequences of accidents are international. The International Atomic Energy Agency (IAEA), based in Vienna, does provide the nuclear industry with a set of safety recommendations, but governments have not agreed to transform them into mandatory obligations. Consequently, the IAEA in unable at present to prevent even gross violations of recommended safety standards at nuclear power plants. It is time for governments to recognize that nuclear technology is too dangerous to be left entirely to the internal discretion of individual nations.

An obvious possibility of redressing this deficiency in the nuclear industry is to enlarge the authority of the IAEA so that it can more effectively supervise the safety of commercial nuclear reactors. Steps in that direction are already being taken and recent experiences have brought to the matter a special sense of urgency. It is presently the practice of the IAEA to send special missions, on invitation, to inspect the operational safety of nuclear plants, although such an exercise is not widespread. We are of the opinion that, as an initial strategy, this procedure must be encouraged and further developed so that confidence established by voluntary inspections facilitates the acceptance of mandatory inspections compatible with sovereign interests. Certain compulsory safety standards should be viewed by governments in a context of self-interest. Without the eventual acceptance of minimum binding obligations, divergent safety standards are bound to evolve, particularly as the nuclear industry expands into developing countries.

Governments must be encouraged to become more amenable to recommendations from the IAEA aimed at increasing the standards of safety at nuclear plants presently under construction and planned for the future. Since accidents are most likely to endanger those living in the immediate area of a nuclear plant, governments should, to the maximum extent, keep new plants far away from densely populated areas and take measures for preventing large human settlements from growing up around them. Steps should also be taken to develop an international licensing system requiring the conformity of new nuclear plants to minimum international standards of safety. These standards will undoubtedly have to be enforced by some inspections which may be politically troublesome owing to sovereign pride or national security. We believe such considerations to be ethically indefensible in the face of threats to human welfare and global safety.

In addition to upgrading technological safety, the IAEA could play a more active role in raising the level of human competency at nuclear plants. Individuals who manage and operate nuclear reactors constitute an important safety factor. Risk studies show that human error accounts for one-third to one-half of all accidents. In this context, the IAEA should endeavour to persuade governments to follow guidelines establishing minimum international qualifications and provide mandatory training and re-training programmes relating to accident prevention and damage containment.

It is noteworthy in this regard that, while governments continue to hedge on accepting minimum international standards for nuclear plants, they have taken swift action on developing an international response in the event of an accident. In a matter of months following the Chernobyl accident, two international conventions concerning an early warning system and multilateral assistance were drafted, adopted and opened for signature. Recognizing the great need for international co-ordination and co-operation in post-accident situations, some 60 States, including all those with nuclear reactors, signed these conventions. The momentum of this progress in international nuclear security must now be channelled into the area of nuclear accident prevention by gathering support for minimum international safety standards.

Nuclear power currently produces only 5 per cent of the world's energy and 15 per cent of its electricity. At global level, the dependence on it is not such that a gradual shift to other sources of energy would prove overly disruptive. However, several industrial countries have made substantial investments and become heavily dependent on nuclear energy, and it would be unrealistic in the short or medium term to expect a radical shift in their energy policies. Given the reality that nuclear power will continue to be a major source of energy for many nations at least for the next two decades, it is imperative that the process of developing an international framework for nuclear accident prevention be accorded the same priority as post-accident co-ordination. The driving force behind national support for international safety standards should be wisdom and foresight, not regret and hindsight in the wake of another nuclear accident.

Coinciding with efforts to introduce international safety standards in the nuclear industry should be a serious programme of eliminating energy waste and increasing efficiency. Inefficient energy use and waste are key barriers to reducing the hazards which stem from reliance on existing sources of energy. Reduction in the use of all forms of energy not only contributes to a safer world and a less polluted environment, but can also increase a country's standard of living. For example, as measured by their gross national products, Sweden and Switzerland consume much less energy per person and have higher standards of living than the United States. It is therefore only prudent that governments inform and educate the general public about energy saving techniques, and promote conservation at all levels.

Ethical Dimensions: The present operation of the nuclear industry calls for an assessment of its ethical dimensions. To what extent are the governments of today bound to take measures to ensure a healthy environment for the generations of tomorrow? Does any country have the moral right to operate technology which has the potential of causing large-scale human suffering and irreparable environmental damage within, as well as beyond, its sovereign territory? How can the conflict between sovereign rights and the global risks posed by nuclear technology be reconciled? Nations must come to grips with these questions before they are overtaken by them.

Scientific innovation has always presented ethical problems, but nuclear technology introduces unique considerations into contemporary codes of conduct. History shows that the development of technology has often taken its toll on human life and the environment. Nuclear technology, however, poses conceivable dangers to human life and the environment on a scale never before imagined. It is imperative, therefore, that governments redefine their responsibility for the safety of our global community.

The humanitarian response to nuclear power is not a sweeping plea for its suspension. Of course, if nuclear technology could easily be replaced by safer, cost-effective sources of energy, considerations of ethics and human survival would dictate its being gradually phased out. The problem is that new sources of energy are decades away from being viable and could yield unforeseen problems and dangers of their own.

We are of the opinion that:

* Sufficient investment of human and financial resources to assess alternative energy sources must be made before determining whether to promote nuclear technology for the future.

* The twin problems of nuclear waste and the decommissioning of nuclear plants must not remain unresolved for too long. It is imperative for all governments with nuclear technology to allocate greater resources in these areas.

* Governments should take steps in a humanitarian context to collaborate on their research in the nuclear field and share their findings. In terms of global responsibilities, each nation must assume its fair share and ensure that further delays in accepting international safety standards for nuclear power are avoided.

Scientific progress need not be forestalled, but if it poses dangers to the international community at large, it must rigorously be made subject to humanitarian constraints.

Genetic Engineering

Advances in bio-technology are opening up new horizons, as yet barely glimpsed, in improving human and animal health, energy and food production. Developments in genetic engineering were sparked by the discovery in 1953 of the chemical structure of DNA – an organic molecule which carries coded within its chemical structure the information for controlling protein synthesis in all living organisms. It thus controls their physical structure, growth reproduction and functioning. Two decades later, further developments enabled scientists to introduce genes from one organism to another to give the recipient the desired characteristics. Through genetic engineering it is proving possible to enhance the nutritional or other values of plants and animals by increasing their product size and the ratio of edible to waste material.

However, before dreaming about re-shaping plants, animals and even human-beings, let us examine what is happening now, for instance in the plant kingdom. Scientists have made very significant progress in recombining genes, but as a result of environmental deterioration, deforestation and new agricultrual practices we are losing thousands of plant species and varieties every year. Genetic combinations and genes themselves, which have taken millions of years to come into existence, are therefore being lost forever. In the future, extraordinary skills to relocate genes from one species to another might be developed. But it will be extremely difficult to anticipate what genetic material will be needed in order to face climatic changes, changes in pests and disease profiles or changes resulting from chemical, biological or nuclear catastrophes.

It is of the utmost importance to understand the silent revolution of gigantic dimensions taking place in the relationship between humankind and nature. For centuries agriculturalists have saved seeds for the next crop after each harvest, thus allowing some of the evolutionary process to proceed through the new genetic combinations resulting from the sexual reproduction taking place in the field. New agricultural technologies have gradually introduced commercial seeds throughout the world, while environmental degradation has contributed to the disappearance of the wild varieties. Co-evolution between cultivated crops and other life forms is no longer possible: evolution continues for the latter, but is being interrupted for the former. Natural diversity influenced by millions of individual decisions of farmers is being replaced by man-made diversity in laboratories and experimental plots, located in just a few decision centres and responding to short-term requirements in terms of yields and profits.

This gradual halting of the evolutionary process affecting cultivated plants has extremely serious consequences for the future of mankind, particularly when it takes place in the areas where the evolutionary process has been historically the most active and the diversity the greatest – in the centres of origin of food crops such as Africa for sorghum, Mexico and Central America for maize, the Middle East for wheat, South and South East Asia for rice, etc. As an example, India has probably grown over 30,000 different varieties of rice over the last half century. Experts predict that, ten years from now, this enormous rice diversity will be reduced to no more than 50 varieties, with the top ten accounting for over three-quarters of the subcontinent's rice acreage. Such a genetic erosion has another consequence: increased genetic uniformity over whole regions makes crops much more vulnerable to possible changes in the environment (climate, pests, diseases, etc.), including those which could be part of biological warfare.

Food crops are essential to the preservation of human life on this planet. They have been domesticated through centuries of empirical observations by the farmers themselves, and only in the last few decades through scientific methods. The most domesticated of all is maize; it cannot survive without human help. New varieties, or even new species, produced by genetic engineering, will be entirely in the hands of large public or private seed corporations. This is already the case with hybrid maize, whose seed has to be bought every year. The seed industry is fast developing thanks to newly enacted plant breeders' rights. Biotechnology will similarly develop if legislation patenting life forms enables firms to make sufficient returns on their research and development investments. Biotechnological advances for food production should therefore be assessed in their economic context, including the fact that new products may not be available at a price poor farmers can afford.

Seed firms are becoming fewer and fewer in number. Those surviving and thriving are powerful multinationals, most of them with agro-chemical interests. Third World leaders who intend to develop a self-sustaining agriculture providing food for all, view the growth of the transnational seed-chemical complexes with great concern. Selling seeds with one hand and pesticides with the other does not trigger research aimed at reducing crop vulnerability to pests and diseases.

Human survival is increasingly dependent on decisions taken by a few profit-oriented firms and a few States viewing plant genetic resources as a national security problem. The international community has come to understand the value of genetic diversity and of its conservation, but has not yet fully grasped the importance of disseminating gene banks in order to promote global food sufficiency and discourage increasing genetic control by a few.

We are of the opinion that:

* Genetic diversity must be protected by various means: as many gene banks as possible, biosphere reserves, botanical gardens, community gardens, etc.

* Farmers, individually or collectively, must also be called upon to protect varieties native to the region, and should be adequately compensated for being the curators of such precious resources.

* Advance bio-technology applied to plant breeding need not be feared if an extensive network is built around the world, based on the human-being as the custodian of diversity and the source of potential creativity existing in all countries, cultures and social groups. This potential creativity should be released not only in laboratories but in the fields through a constant interaction of farmers with scientists.

* In view of the recent advances in so far as manipulation of animal and human genes is concerned, it is most urgent and important for governments to study rigorously the humanitarian implications before major scientific research and experimentation projects are undertaken.

* Bio-ethics must keep pace with technological innovations. Scientific progress and technological breakthroughs lose much

169

of their value if their relevance to human well-being is not clearly established. This is why we are convinced that human wisdom must not lag behind human knowledge.

Industrial Disasters

Industrial accidents are not new phenomena but their scale and the dangers they threaten are unprecedented. Factories producing dangerous chemicals are now bigger than ever; the processing methods have become more complex; and the number of chemical products has grown. Most important of all, the number of potential victims of any accident – people living within the danger zone – has risen dramatically. This is because urbanization, particularly in the Third World, has brought many more people into the vicinity of industrial zones, and because the chemicals themselves have become more hazardous, endangering the inhabitants of a wider area than before.

These factors have made industrial accidents more difficult to deal with and more extensive in their damage. Furthermore, they often have little-known and long-lasting effects on the environments they pollute and the people they poison. In some cases the illnesses may be detected years after the accident in people who lived outside what was then claimed to be the danger zone.

The hazard of industrial disasters is increasing with time, not only because of proliferation of major plants, but also because many factories built in the 1950s and 1960s are now ageing. Due to lack of rigorous control and maintenance, especially in developing countries, the risk has proportionally increased.

We believe that it is vital to identify methodically the risk areas and hazards involved and to take measures to minimize the damage to human life and property.

We recommend that:

* Measures be taken to ensure that full access to information concerning chemical plants is available to all interested parties, including local authorities and populations living in the areas surrounding industrial plants.

* The storage of dangerous chemicals and the regular inspection of

installations should be subject to rigorous international standards.

* High-risk chemical plants should not be located in densely populated areas and governments should take strict measures to remove unauthorized urban migrants from the risk zones around industrial plants.

* At national, regional and international level, including the United Nations, monitoring systems as well as emergency plans should be developed for the safety of people.

Disaster Management

Statistics of the last few years show that, despite technological progress and the unprecedented means now available to prevent loss of life and contain material damage, the number of disaster victims is steadily increasing. More than one million people are estimated to have died in natural disasters during the period 1970 to 1981 and damage in excess of $46 billion was caused. Every indication is that disasters will increase and claim greater numbers of lives in the future. A global humanitarian consensus invariably emerges in major crisis situations to alleviate human suffering. But there has been a failure at all levels to mould this goodwill into effective and coherent policies to prevent, prepare for and respond to disasters.

The degree to which a particular occurrence constitutes a disaster, sufficient to warrant an international response, is determined in relation to such factors as the resources locally available to deal with its consequences, the accessibility of the affected areas, and community experience in dealing with such situations. Attempts to define disasters in terms of casualties and material damage seldom prove useful unless they take sufficient account of local conditions. An event constituting a major disaster in an unprepared or poor country may pass unheralded in other nations which have the means and practical knowledge to deal with similar calamities on a regular basis.

Disasters requiring an international humanitarian response occur on average once every three weeks. They sometimes inflict irreparable damage on communities and tear apart the social fabric of whole societies. Yet most disasters are in large

171

measure man-made and can be contained, if not prevented by man. Although they may be precipitated by natural forces, the majority of disasters striking those who are least able to cope with them are structurally linked to hazardous patterns of socio-economic development and environmental degradation. During an earthquake, for example, those residing in poorly constructed buildings are the most vulnerable.

Categories of Disasters: The line between natural and man-made disasters has become increasingly blurred. However, in order to evaluate the existing framework for disaster management, identify lacunae and provide constructive recommendations, it may be helpful to separate disasters into four categories:

(i) Elemental: for example, earthquakes, tidal waves, floods, volcanic eruptions and landslides. These are distinguished from other disasters because they are instantaneous and prompted by climatic or geological forces. Their destructiveness depends more on the number of vulnerable people in a given area than on their inherent severity. In many parts of the world, man-made errors exacerbate the damage they cause.

(ii) Foreseeable: for example, famines and epidemics. These have complex root causes in which climatic and human activity interact over extended periods, leaving large numbers of people vulnerable. This interaction creates a vicious circle whose recurrence is often predictable.

(iii) Deliberate: for example, results of wars between States, civil wars, guerrilla warfare and insurgency activity.

(iv) Accidental: for example, industrial and nuclear catastrophes. These are a by-product of technological advances in the twentieth century. The recent accidents of Bhopal and Chernobyl attest to the threat posed by such disasters.

International Framework for Disaster Management: Recent research, supported by field data and experience at the grass roots level, demonstrates that neither conventional wisdom nor existing response mechanisms are adequate to face the growing challenge of disasters. The current international system of disaster management is increasingly becoming a non-system owing to chaotic organization, as well as duplication and waste due to the proliferation of *ad hoc* bodies which are keen to help but unco-ordinated and ineffective in responding to real needs. At the heart of the problem, is the fact that the international community has failed to construct a viable *modus operandi* for dealing effectively with the humanitarian dimensions of disasters.

Theoretically, the United Nations system possesses the institutional and material capacity for effective disaster management on an international scale. Its response, however, has often been marred by internal problems of co-ordination and fallen short of the imperative need for swift and appropriate action. Instead of marshalling their efforts to maximize the impact of the United Nations system as a whole, its various components such as the International Atomic Energy Agency (IAEA), Food and Agriculture Organization (FAO), World Food Programme (WFP), United Nations Development Programme (UNDP), United Nations High Commission for Refugees (UNHCR), and United Nations Children's Fund (UNICEF), which hold mandates for different types of disasters, have focused on their own sectoral priorities and programmes. There is no central co-ordinating body within the United Nations bringing to a disaster the full potential of its technical capability and material resources.

In 1971, the United Nations General Assembly established the United Nations Disaster Relief Office (UNDRO) with the mandate to mobilize, direct and co-ordinate international disaster relief efforts and to promote disaster prevention, planning and preparedness. However, the Office needs to be considerably strengthened in order to establish its leadership vis-à-vis other major agencies of the United Nations system which have considerably larger human and financial resources. Of the four broad categories of disasters outlined above, UNDRO covers only one: the elemental. Other disasters in the three remaining categories are only partly covered in a haphazard manner by different bodies of the United Nations.

In our view, this amorphous international framework for

disaster management leads to poor co-ordination and inappro-priate responses. There is a tendency for organizations to neglect policies of prevention and preparedness and address disasters only after they occur. As it is presently administered, disaster relief has been criticized as 'quick-fix' therapy which wastes resources that otherwise might have been used to resolve the root causes of a disaster. Too often, disaster relief has led to a dehumanizing dependency upon others for survival because it fails to include programmes for rehabilitation. It is often ill-adapted to local needs and insensitive to the habits, culture and traditions of the victims. This affects negatively the credibility of aid agencies and donor governments which are blamed for dumping their surpluses rather than responding to the needs of victims. There is little effort to date to ensure, as a matter of principle, full local participation in disaster management strategies or to gather local knowledge for centralized data banks in order to facilitate speedy and effective responses.

A rapid and effective response to disaster depends upon accurate and detailed information reaching international organizations responsible for humanitarian assistance. Until recently, information has been poor in quality and slow to reach the competent authorities. However, a number of factors are changing this pattern. Satellites are being used to assess variations in climate and vegetation cover and can help forewarn of impending drought or food shortage. There is a greater use of computers to evaluate complex inter-related variables and make predictions. Probably most important of all is the growing awareness by those involved in disaster management of the importance of the local knowledge of people living and working in the threatened areas. Humanitarian behaviour is decisive in mitigating or aggravating the damage. Early warning systems should include this factor as a vital component.

The Political Factor: Systemic failures in the international network for disaster management are compounded by the existence of political manoeuvring on the part of disaster-stricken countries as well as prospective donor governments. There is a propensity on all fronts for sovereign prerogatives to prevail over humanitarian disaster management. There may, for example, be genuine ambiguity in determining when a chronic food shortage becomes a famine. But too often, governments concerned with internal political stability and other related factors have chosen to forego the mobilization of national and international relief rather than acknowledge that a disaster has occurred. Without a government's acknowledgement that it needs help, most international response mechanisms are immobilized in the face of needless human suffering. Political considerations on the part of donor governments have also sometimes worked to obstruct sorely needed disaster assistance. Provision of food, medical and material aid by donor governments is often more dependent on the recipient's political orientations than on the extent of human need. No effective legal constraints are in force at the international level to ensure the predominance of humanitarian over political considerations.

National Frameworks for Disaster Management: Most national governments, particularly those of disaster-prone countries, have done little to enhance their own disaster-response capabilities in order to prevent or mitigate the debilitating effects of disasters. Studies indicate that countries where disasters strike most often are among the least prepared to respond. Many governments are without national disaster strategies and concomitant disaster management institutions to ensure optimal use of local resources and secure unhindered access for international relief in the event of a disaster. It may be that the most vulnerable countries feel they cannot afford to allocate severely limited resources to disaster prevention and preparedness schemes. But it is clear that national disaster management strategies are crucial if there is to be any hope of breaking the debilitating cycle of poverty and disaster.

Humanitarian Code of Conduct: We believe that the first requirement for a more effective approach to disaster management at both the international and national levels is a greater appreciation of the relationship between the elements in the disaster management continuum – prevention, preparedness, relief and rehabilitation – on the one hand, and the humanitarian priorities of saving lives and mitigating human suffering on the other. The foundation for a framework in which to fit the multiple responses required of governments and international and national organizations lies in the recognition that humanitarian criteria must at least mitigate and hopefully prevail over the constraints of politics and sovereignty, particularly during the limited emergency period. The elaboration and acceptance in law of a humanitarian code of conduct will help pave the way for overcoming many of the problems which currently plague disaster management efforts.

Adherence to humanitarian principles in disaster management will serve to clarify the context of disasters and re-order priorities around the human-being. The recognition of structural links between disasters and socio-economic development will necessitate a review of certain developmental policies and practices. Incorporating humanitarian considerations into revised policies and practices by including strategies for self-reliance within relief programmes and by utilizing local participation in all phases of disaster management promises not only to ensure the most appropriate response in a given situation, but also to preserve and enhance human dignity. It is increasingly clear that it is not the inherent severity of the disaster but the vulnerability of the victims which counts most in developing effective disaster management strategies.

United Nations Co-ordination: Reliance upon humanitarian principles for disaster management at the national and international level must be coupled with a plan to bring together different United Nations bodies under one leadership for a pre-determined period of time in order to co-ordinate and optimize the capabilities and resources of the United Nations system as a whole. Whether the mandate of UNDRO is enlarged or a small body is established to take on this responsibility, the proposed entity should have the requisite authority to declare a disaster and co-ordinate United Nations staff and resources during the response period. It should maintain a central repository of information relating to all phases of disaster management and draw upon the resources of existing bodies for an effective early-warning system. Once the entity has determined, on the basis of well-defined criteria, that a disaster has occurred or is likely to occur, it would then request the UN Secretary-General to declare an emergency situation for a limited period of time and activate a co-ordinated response. At the same time, the entity would have to work closely with governments and NGOs concerned with the emergency so that responses on all fronts are co-ordinated and complementary. A timely, co-ordinated international response of this kind is desperately needed to bring about the maximum alleviation of human suffering in disaster situations. Moreover, an effective response by the United Nations in this high profile field of disaster management would enhance its credibility with the media and governments and promote an extension of its reach in promoting human welfare.

A unified and co-ordinated approach guided by humanitarian principles to disaster management on all fronts has yet to become a reality, but its urgency cannot be denied. Owing to the squandering of natural resources, ill-planned urbanization, over-industrialization, distorted demographic growth, the proliferation of potentially dangerous technology and uneven patterns of socio-economic development, the coming decades are all too likely to be punctuated with the scourge of disasters unless a holistic, humanitarian strategy for disaster management is adopted. Incorporating humanitarian principles into the prevention phase of disaster management can also be a catalyst in helping vulnerable communities break out of the relentless poverty–disaster–poverty cycle. In view of the fact that no nation is immune to the potential threat of a large-scale disaster of one kind or another, it is in everyone's self-interest to support a humanitarian approach to disaster management.

We recommend that:

* ★ The United Nations should elaborate and promote a special legal, administrative, financial and operational code of conduct to regulate the management of disasters. The cornerstone of the code should be the increasingly recognized principle that, during a disaster, humanitarian criteria ought to prevail over any political or sovereignty constraints for the limited period of the emergency. In practice, this will include concepts such as 'mercy corridors' entailing, to the extent compatible with minimum standards of hygiene and national security, relaxed procedures

177

for the entry of relief personnel and import of goods to ensure unhindered access of assistance to victims.

* The United Nations should designate a central co-ordinating body which is fully recognized as *primus inter pares* for a predetermined period of time bringing to a disaster the full potential of the international network. It should have acknowledged authority to declare a disaster and to intervene effectively.

* The designated entity should draw upon existing systems; adjust them to the requirements of each disaster category; monitor disaster-prone areas on a continuing basis; and make timely suggestions for disaster preparedness.

* Once the entity is satisfied on the basis of well-defined criteria that a disaster has occurred or is about to occur, it should request the United Nations Secretary-General to declare an emergency situation for a limited period of time. This should be determined according to the nature of the disaster, the place, the circumstances and the requirements of the situation.

* During the disaster period, the entity should have the authority to co-ordinate the receipt and disbursement of emergency funds based on pre-arranged formulae with donors and recipient officials and be empowered to establish priorities after assessing actual human needs. It should also have recognized authority to co-ordinate emergency relief provided by inter-governmental and non-governmental bodies concerned for a pre-determined period in order to ensure complementary responses.

* The entity should work closely with governments, particularly the disaster-prone nations, in formulating strategies to prevent disasters and in developing a pre-established *modus operandi* to ensure optimal use of local material and human resources in the event of a disaster. Bilateral legal commitments between the UN entity and governments establishing the extent of the entity's authority within a nation's sovereign territory should be considered to facilitate reception and distribution of relief.

* This entity should maintain a central repository for information relating to all phases of disaster management: prevention, preparedness, relief and rehabilitation. National disaster assistance offices and humanitarian organizations should provide all relevant information, particularly general accounts of practical problems actually encountered in these areas, for inclusion in the data bank.

* The latter should maintain an up-to-date register of monitoring, communications and transportation technologies for effective surveillance of disasters as well as prompt delivery of personnel, equipment and supplies to the disaster area.

* The United Nations should launch an education campaign sensitizing governments and the international community to the inter-relationships of disasters, poverty, underdevelopment, burgeoning populations and environmental degradation. Pro- grammes of disaster management should establish closer links between these areas in their planning and implementation.

* The United Nations should develop an effective media strategy which serves, on the one hand, to warn local people and decision- makers of impending disasters and, on the other, to lay the basis for accurate, long-term information on the causes and effects of disasters. This strategy will enable humanitarian action to be more visible to both recipient and donor governments, thereby enhancing the credibility of the United Nations and its constituent agencies which depends as much on the public perception and media coverage of their action as on the speed and effectiveness with which it is taken.

* Governments without national disaster plans or concomitant disaster institutions should re-think their priorities and allocate resources to fill this lacuna in their structure. Where appropriate, governments should be provided with technical and financial means to do so.

* Governments which have advanced surveillance and communica- tions systems should examine the means by which information relevant to all phases of disaster management can be gathered and made available to concerned countries via the designated entity so that swift humanitarian action can be taken.

* Governments, humanitarian organizations and the international community should promote the progressive development of international law whereby States are obligated: to prepare for disaster relief within their own territory and to take preventive measures to minimize suffering resulting from disasters; to accept relief for their people from the international community after the occurrence of a disaster, if their own resources are inadequate; and to make efforts in good faith to assist another State in the event of a disaster.

* There should be greater reliance on disaster impact analysis by

179

researchers and field-workers with direct personal experience of disaster situations in order to identify the key elements for disaster management programmes and to establish the most humane, yet pragmatic, priorities. Greater weight should be accorded to people with field experience in data gathering.

* Disaster management programmes of prevention, preparedness, relief and rehabilitation must, at least in part, be devised and applied by insiders at the local level for optimal efficiency and sensitivity. Food consumption habits, traditional medicines, religious values and other local customs of communities should be researched for each phase of disaster management in order to avoid programmes which are inappropriate or demeaning to the culture of the people in need.

* Donor governments, in collaboration with disaster-prone countries and the United Nations system, should help build stocks in strategically located areas in order to ensure ready availability of relief. Such stocks should consist not only of foodstuffs, medicines and other articles needed in emergencies but also of spare parts for vehicles and other appropriate materials which facilitate logistics in emergency situations.

* The initial welfare phase of disaster response should give way as quickly as possible to programmes of rehabilitation and development to facilitate self-reliance for the preservation and enhancement of human dignity. Implementing income-generating programmes should have the dual purpose of guarding against a debilitating dependency upon others for survival and securing a better base from which to ward off the worst effects of the next disaster.

We recognize that many of these functions are already more or less assumed by existing inter-governmental agencies such as UNDRO and WFP and by non-governmental bodies like the League of the Red Cross and Crescent Societies and other major voluntary agencies. We urge that their human and financial resources be strengthened. Donor governments should provide for, as a few already do, special allocations that can be made at short notice when a disaster occurs. Early warning systems, immediate sharing of information with victims as well as neighbouring communities or countries, and the application of a comprehensive code of conduct, as mentioned above, should be a part of the package. This is particularly relevant in the case of the new man-made disasters that we have referred to earlier in this chapter.

PART III
THE HOPE

7. General Conclusions and Recommendations

*"It was the best of times, it was the worst of times,
it was the age of wisdom, it was the age of foolishness,
it was the epoch of belief, it was the epoch of incredulity,
it was the season of light, it was the season of darkness,
it was the spring of hope, it was the winter of despair."*

Charles Dickens, 1859

Our purpose in preparing this Report was principally to rescue hope from the dismal, complex and increasingly confusing environment in which we live. We do not wish to be prophets of gloom and doom because we do not believe it is desirable or justified. Nor do we wish to be unduly optimistic because that would be wrong and misleading. There is no easily available panacea for the ills that afflict contemporary society. In the humanitarian field, as complex as it is neglected, there can be no short-cuts, no quick-fixes, no ready-made blueprints for global action. Reaffirming faith in the basic human impulses which have ensured our survival and progress is, however, essential. Hope is one of those impulses. And humankind needs to nurture and strengthen it in this age more than ever before in its history.

Addressing humanitarian problems is a challenge to the mind as well as to the heart. We recognize the limitations of our endeavour. We realize also that feelings and thoughts in themselves are not a substitute for action. But that is where action begins. As we analysed the humanitarian issues on our agenda, one after the other, we realized more and more that, within the limited time frame of our Commission, we would be able to do no more than scratch the surface of the humanitarian paradigm. We also realized that no declarations, resolutions or reports would help in the humanitarian field unless and until individuals and nations alike decide to help themselves in making their social environment more humane. High-minded intentions are not enough and are no substitute for a meaningful programme of action.

The Hope

Being humanitarian is a responsibility which human-beings are finding increasingly difficult to assume in the present social, economic and political environment. But if people, whether paralysed by poverty or dazzled by abundance, would allow themselves to be humane, many of their problems would become easier to solve. We see humanitarianism as the bridge between ethics and human rights, both of which are needed to make global society healthy and secure for the present and future generations.

By choosing to concentrate on some specific humanitarian issues of direct and daily relevance to human well-being, we have attempted to demonstrate the practical side of humanitarianism. Even if our effort serves only as a catalyst for further work on issues we have dealt with and others equally deserving of attention, it will not have been in vain.

That humankind today has within its power the capacity to annihilate all forms of life just as much as it has the means to lead global society to a prosperity unprecedented in history, is for us a sign of hope, not despair. For we believe that, in the end, only those human impulses which ensure survival and well-being will prevail. It is on faith in human nature that we have built the hope which is the message of this Report.

To strengthen hope, the foremost task for peoples and nations is to nurture *multilateralism*. Recent years have witnessed its steady retreat before the short-term benefits that unilateralism and bilateralism bring. We consider multilateralism, of which the United Nations and other international institutions are the building blocks, essential to man's future.

More than ever before, the choices faced by people throughout the world are being determined by the actions of others in far distant places. The decisions we take as to what we buy, eat, wear or how we live, the environmental consequences of the energy we consume or how we dispose of waste, have ramifications not just for our immediate family, neighbours and national society, but for the global community as a whole as well as future generations. It is no longer possible to pretend that people can live in isolation from each other.

It is, of course, easy for the rich and the powerful few to dismiss lightly or disregard the notion of a global community. For the poor and the weak, the majority of humankind, it is a reality which adds a new dimension to their vulnerability. Despite widespread poverty and hunger, resources are squandered without thought of their renewal, and huge sums are invested in weapons of mass destruction. The weak are sacrificed as pawns in the games of the powerful, but their increasing numbers and rising discontent threaten the very foundations of the global social structure.

The fact that the failure to address a given conflict could have global repercussions compels recognition of the need to resolve international conflicts through negotiation and compromise. Time and again, it has proven futile to rely on unilateral solutions when contemporary problems demand a multilateral approach.

The present framework for the conduct of international relations on a multilateral basis was established in the Charter of the United Nations. Those who created the Charter were optimistic that 'We the Peoples' could co-operate to ensure economic and social justice, equal rights, and peace through collective security for all. At various levels progress has been substantial. The United Nations has been instrumental in the process of decolonization; it has fostered development programmes and economic growth; its peace-keeping efforts, though not as frequent or extensive as envisaged in the Charter, have helped stabilize some troubled areas; and it has expanded or strengthened international law concerning a wide range of global concerns.

Humanitarian issues have been identified and addressed. Efforts have been made to enhance international co-operation to improve the environment, eliminate racial discrimination, enhance the status of women, regulate population growth and afford greater protection for children, minorities, refugees, displaced persons and others at risk. A complex institutional network has evolved to facilitate international co-operation on these issues. However, the benefits to people throughout the world have fallen far short of the recommendations, resolutions and rhetoric of internationalism. It has proved immensely difficult to move beyond idealistic commitments and the invocation of universal values to apply them in an imperfect world.

Governments, increasingly conscious of their limitations,

have tended to react defensively, decrying the failure of multilateralism, threatening and sometimes implementing drastic reductions in their funding of multilateral organizations. However unjustified, such items are understandable. International institutions commonly suffer from bureaucratic expansion, which produces overlapping responsibilities and confusion about organizational objectives and priorities. Nor is there always a willingness among bureaucrats in different agencies to co-operate to ensure prompt and trenchant action in crisis situations. International institutions are inclined to adopt a paternalistic approach to humanitarian problems, and pass over local knowledge in favour of sterile, textbook solutions or outside 'experts', often at great expense and with unsatisfactory results.

Institutional efforts tend to fall short of their potential, thus encouraging a "we can do better" attitude on the part of individual governments, which then use this as a pretext to opt out of multilateral arrangements. The fault, however, does not lie entirely with the failure of international institutions. There has been a tendency to expect too much from them and to ignore the inherent scope and limits of their policies and actions.

The problems faced by multilateralism are multiple. The establishment of an international community based upon freely negotiated agreement between sovereign States is recent history. Formerly, international arrangements were the result of strong States imposing their will on weaker States. Following the demise of the League of Nations and the terrible devastation wrought by the Second World War, the founders of the United Nations realized the need to create a new world order based on humanitarian principles and international law.

Disagreements about what were to be the guiding aims of the United Nations were initially minimal. The resulting consensus, however, inevitably excluded wider sources of influence. Problems which were to accompany the emergence of newly independent States on the global political stage, requiring a whole redefinition of mutual understanding and co-operation, had not yet materialized.

As the United Nations Organization grew from its original 51 members to include some 160 States, many of which had little experience of global politics, the consensus on which it was based began to erode. Some argue that this consensus was always illusory, because the concept of world order envisaged in the UN Charter was that of a community of nations perceived to be equal irrespective of their size and influence, when the international reality is one of inequality of wealth, power and levels of development. Given the success of various multilateral undertakings which have evolved out of this consensus, such arguments are perhaps too extreme. Nevertheless, the failure to take into account deep-seated differences among member States has led to certain incongruities.

The United Nations is a forum where all countries, regardless of their size, can voice opinions and take part in international decision-making. Within this framework, small States can unite on a certain position and thereby influence the development of events and the attitude of powerful States. However, the real influence of smaller States has been minimal. Although voting at the UN may go one way, decisions of consequence are likely to go another, with the result that humanitarian principles and international law are sometimes only selectively observed and applied.

Governments have sought to confine humanitarian concerns to the periphery of international relations, thus precluding interaction and dialogue on issues of fundamental relevance to humankind. The tendency to do this reflects a continuing attachment to the State as the basic unit in the mosaic of global networks, and a reluctance to examine the ambiguities, complexities and dangers inherent in contemporary global society.

National and regional leanings coupled with the existence of ideological blocs readily lend themselves to oversimplified conceptions of the world. Locating issues in the context of adversarial relations inhibits co-operation for the purpose of accommodating differences and solving pressing humanitarian problems. The latitude for compassion is rigidly constricted by the longitude of political or ideological competition.

Although the changing times call for a modification in the traditional concept of the State, it is unrealistic to expect that it will not remain the basic unit of international relations in the near future. Even the UN Charter specifically recognizes the concept of state sovereignty and discourages intervention in States' internal affairs. It is in the common interest of all States to uphold the UN system, but that will not always impel them to an unlimited acceptance of common interests if these conflict with particular ones. Sometimes the interests of participating States are marginal, if not actually contradictory to multilateral objectives. In such cases, States often behave hypocritically and, in the absence of effective sanctions, do so with impunity.

However, sovereignty need not conflict with humanitarian concerns if States can be brought to define their interests beyond the short term. Trimming the edges of sovereignty to allow for effective multilateralism does not imply undermining or superseding the State. The interests of common humanity which transcend national boundaries are not a menace to the vital interests of States.

In the multilateral institutions which have evolved over the last four decades, we can already see a framework which is destined both to subsume and satisfy the nationalisms of the past. Presently there are serious problems with the United Nations and other multilateral institutions. But it is worth remembering that multilateralism, like diversity, can be a source of enrichment rather than a constraint. Existing institutions should be seen not as the end but the beginning of a global process. Truly effective mechanisms for the accommodation of diverse interests can only come into being after extended prior experience. It takes time and effort to develop equitable problem-solving procedures and a consensus which can serve as the cornerstone of international decision-making.

We are convinced of the need for global consensus-building and for strengthening multilateralism. We realize that powerful and privileged States with a vested interest in preserving the status quo are less likely to gain immediate benefits from multilateral arrangements. It is therefore to be expected that, in the absence of far-sighted policies, their consent or acquiescence in the initiatives of a weaker majority may tend to be reluctant and minimal. Weaker States, on the other hand, may well be suspicious of the motives of the major powers. Nonetheless, there are ways of encouraging the evolution of a genuine multilateral consensus.

In order to reconcile conflicts of interest among nations,

individuals must be engaged in collective action at all levels, not only formally as members of international bodies such as the UN, but as actual participants in the consensus upon which multilateralism relies. Persons are unlikely to observe norms set by the international community until they believe themselves to be active subjects rather than passive objects of international laws and practices.

Unless due regard is demonstrated for persons and for the things they care most about, they will have little motivation for participating in collective arrangements to promote human welfare. The more their self-esteem is strengthened by institutions, the more they will be motivated to support those institutions for the sake of their own advantage, and the more likely it is that they will respect one another.

The classic approach to building a consensus out of diversity is to educate citizens throughout the world in the meaning, value and advantage of adhering to humanitarian principles and international law. Textbooks for school children, accessible literature for adults and popular media projects could all be used to strengthen respect for international norms and principles. General awareness of these principles and the knowledge that rational persons are prepared to act on them will enhance understanding and the support of the public. Widely disseminated humanitarian values can also provide a common basis for considering different points of view and evaluating them impartially in order to make more informed decisions and avoid costly errors.

The construction of a more effective framework for the management of global problems demands a greater degree of flexibility and innovation on the part of multilateral institutions. For it is not only necessary to devise and agree upon possible solutions, but to apply those solutions in the proper context. Too often, the pluralist nature of the world community is not given due consideration. Instead there is an unfortunate tendency to espouse a misconceived globalism according to which uniform, theoretical solutions are preferred over local, practical ones. The reluctance to abandon established approaches to multilateral problems is understandable, particularly when it is difficult and time-consuming to persuade concerned parties to agree upon innovative solutions. However, there are at least two senses in which uniform global solutions are inappropriate.

In the first place, people live in communities within nations and each has its own characteristics and possibilities. When they are beset by large-scale problems, it is often necessary to appeal to the international community as a whole for assistance. But if that assistance is to be effective in enabling the full realization of human needs, differences in historical, cultural, religious and ethnic background, geographical circumstance and levels of development must be taken into account.

Moreover, not all large-scale problems are best addressed by appeals to the entire international community. Many successful multilateral activities have occurred at a regional rather than global level. Admittedly, regional efforts complement but cannot substitute for the multilateral network of the United Nations. Multilateralism is synonymous not with uniform global solutions, but with many-sided participation in problem-solving. International, regional and local communities must work together to complement and reinforce efforts to promote human welfare.

To arrest the erosion of faith in multilateralism, the policy-makers within international institutions must evaluate the consequences of their policies in the widest possible sense. In the past, inadequate attention was paid to the context of multilateral projects, their suitability, the claims of competing values and the humanitarian impact of recommended measures, with the result that progress, particularly in social terms, was seldom cost-effective. Given the budgetary constraints within which governments must operate, it is unlikely that sufficient funding for the United Nations and other multilateral agencies will be restored unless international institutions demonstrate to the community of nations that their donations are well spent. In some cases, this will require fundamental reforms in institutions, including the necessary structural changes to adapt to new problems, improved management and leadership at all levels, and strategies to ensure that conferences and meetings are well-planned and necessary.

Additional attempts must be made to distribute the financial burden of supporting international institutions more equitably.

When only a few of the many countries belonging to an organization provide a disproportionate share of its funding, there is a propensity for those countries to exercise undue influence over the direction of its affairs. If multilateralism is not to be used as a front for the powerful, present arrangements relating to financial responsibility must be reviewed.

International institutions would do well to launch a public relations campaign to document the valuable role they play in world affairs. Conceivably such a campaign could help adjust governments' expectations to a more realistic level and marshall grassroots support for multilateral undertakings. Governments and private individuals can be made to realize that the painstakingly slow progress in formulating multilateral solutions to global problems is reason for hope rather than despair.

The deficiencies in contemporary multilateral mechanisms cannot be denied, but neither can the compelling need for multilateral forums where nations and other international actors can address common problems. The imperfections of multilateralism recall us to our duty of improvement and advancement, which is no more than self-improvement and self-advancement. For multilateral institutions are not abstract entities, but a larger reflection of ourselves and the state of our relations with others.

★   ★   ★

In the preceding chapters of this Report, we have made a series of recommendations relating to the humanitarian issues we examined. Our Sectoral Reports, which have been published separately, contain greater details for those who may be interested in any of the specific issues. It is our hope that governments, as well as inter-governmental and non-governmental organizations, will take them into consideration in their policy-making processes and build upon them through further research and reflection.

In concluding this Report, we wish, however, to make some general recommendations which, in our view, would help improve the overall human condition:

193

★ With regard to our own work, we feel that an active follow-up is called for. We have decided, for this purpose, to establish for a limited period **An Independent Bureau for Humanitarian Issues**. Its task will be to complete the publication of the Sectoral Reports on the subjects we examined and to undertake their dissemination, particularly in the developing countries where humanitarian problems are most acute. The Bureau will also undertake appropriate follow-up activities with governments, international and regional organizations and non-governmental agencies so that tangible results are achieved in terms of humanitarian policies and practices.

★ We are convinced that it would be useful for countries to establish **Independent National Commissions** to look into those humanitarian issues which have remained neglected within a national context. A beginning could be made by taking up relevant issues which we have dealt with in a global context. Such Commissions, which could take the form of legal non-governmental, non-profit-making humanitarian entities, could have a collective impact on the efforts world-wide to improve the human condition. If established in all regions, they could together form the nucleus of a **humanitarian movement** that would complement the existing bodies and on-going efforts in the humanitarian field by promoting issues which are inadequately addressed and by filling the gaps in the existing body of humanitarian law and practice.

★ With regard to official action, we recommend that governments consider the possibility of establishing, at the policy-making level within the official infrastructure, an entity with adequate power and authority, to be responsible for humanitarian issues. Ideally, it would be desirable to create **A Ministry of Humanitarian Affairs** or a special department attached to the office of the Head of State or Government. Such a ministry or department would be responsible for analysing, in a rigorous and systematic manner, the implications for human-beings of proposed policies in the social, economic, security and other fields. At present, humanitarian issues are variously the concern of the Ministries of Interior, Social Welfare, Justice, and Foreign Affairs.

Compartmentalization puts such issues at a disadvantage vis-à-vis other matters which have their specific advocates within the cabinet. The proposed entity would bring cohesion into the complex and diverse humanitarian networks and ensure that humanitarianism becomes a factor in the national policy-making process on a par with other factors which currently play a decisive role in policy formulation. It would also serve as the focal point for effective co-ordination within the governmental structure of concerted responses to humanitarian problems. It would have a holistic multi-disciplinary approach, taking fully into account the inter-linkages. It would thus play an important role in articulating a cohesive response to the demands and pressures of specific humanitarian lobbies represented by various humanitarian inter-governmental and non-governmental organizations. One benefit of such an approach would be a more equitable and appropriate distribution of scarce financial resources allocated to the resolution of diverse humanitarian problems.

★ We recognize that most humanitarian problems would become less acute if fundamental **human rights** were respected. Although the field of human rights has its own specificity and has been only indirectly a part of our work, we consider it of utmost importance to strengthen human rights at the national, regional and international level. The United Nations Charter recognizes human rights as one of its major concerns. It would be helpful if a much higher level of human and financial resources were allocated to the protection and promotion of human rights.

★ At the same time, the United Nations should consider the possibility of establishing a UN **Central Office for Humanitarian Issues**, close to the Secretary-General, just as has been done for economic and development issues. Such an office, small but effective, with functions distinct from human rights, would be helpful in co-ordinating policies and programmes of the United Nations system, maximizing their impact, and in monitoring as well as providing policy guidance in regard to specific humanitarian issues, including in particular those which are not adequately covered by existing agencies. Those specialized agencies whose work has a direct relevance to humanitarian issues should have within their structures designated departments or officials whose duties should include continuous liaison with the proposed central office. The latter could also serve as the principal interlocutor vis-à-vis governments in cases of humanitarian emergencies, particularly in areas uncovered or inadequately covered by existing bodies.

★ In the case of humanitarian assistance, we note that a relatively high proportion of it is devoted to relief activities and temporary

195

measures as compared to permanent solutions of humanitarian problems. We urge international organizations and governments to pay greater attention to root causes and structural changes which would help eliminate them. We are firmly of the view that international efforts should be concentrated, in the first place, on **prevention** rather than cure. We have pleaded for this approach in all of the specific humanitarian issues we examined and which are subjects of special Sectoral Reports mentioned earlier.

* In situations of emergency, we firmly believe that humanitarian priorities should prevail over political considerations. Much too often, relief aid and human suffering are used to promote certain political objectives. This is an aberration against which the international community should collectively act whenever and wherever it occurs. While respecting the sovereign prerogatives of States, we believe that these should make room for humanitarian concerns in situations of emergency. Adequate measures should be taken to enable victims to have access to humanitarian aid, whatever their social or political affiliation. In situations of armed conflict, humanitarian organizations should be granted mercy corridors in order to reach the victims speedily. Special measures should be taken to protect children, women and the aged. In order to systematize the wide-ranging field of humanitarian emergencies and the aid provided, we recommend that States consider the articulation of **A Right to Humanitarian Assistance** which should have adequate, mutually agreed, legally binding content as to the principles and practices that should govern action in situations of humanitarian emergencies.

* With regard to international humanitarian law which received our special attention, we note that at present it is directed essentially to humanizing war. While commending the noble and essential activities undertaken in the context of the Red Cross movement and, in particular, the work of the International Committee of the Red Cross, we feel that the concept of international humanitarian law should be broadened to include **The Law of Peace** relating to human welfare in situations constituting a serious threat to human life, dignity and welfare. Already in the existing body of law, problems such as refugees, missing persons and the disappeared are included. This trend should be encouraged in order to broaden its scope. The linkage between international humanitarian law and the law of human rights should be highlighted and further articulated. As a first step, it would be useful to elaborate **A Declaration containing the**

minimum humanitarian principles, based on universally accepted values common to world cultures, movements and religions. The identification of such points of convergence in the human family would be a positive step towards strengthening the human solidarity which humanitarian issues call for. It will also serve as a cornerstone for the promotion of confidence-building measures in the humanitarian field and contribute to an improvement in the global social climate.

★ In the case of international financial institutions, we are of the opinion that their policies and programmes should include social development among their top priorities. They should also show greater sensitivity to the special needs of vulnerable groups, including those we have referred to in this Report, and influence governments accordingly. We note that the World Bank's policies are already evolving in this direction and commend them to other related bodies as well as regional development banks. We recommend that these should undertake social and environmental studies before approving grants and loans and should ensure the fullest co-operation of the local, affected populations.

★ At present, in the field of advanced research, a disproportionately high percentage of government funds and grants from the private sector are devoted to the natural rather than the social sciences. No wonder man's knowledge of himself has lagged behind his knowledge of matter. We recommend that more human and financial resources be allocated to research in the social sciences and humanities, including particularly those fields related to humanitarian issues which have practical implications for the social and political well-being of countries.

★ The education systems of most countries are likewise geared to the natural sciences. While we recognize the importance of learning subjects which relate directly to the requirements of the labour market, we feel it is important for governments and educational institutions to review syllabuses in order to provide more space for humanitarian issues. At school and university in particular, it would be useful to introduce them as subjects of study.

★ We also recommend that the United Nations, with the technical assistance of its Educational, Scientific and Cultural Organization (UNESCO), should develop in consultation with educationalists of member States, a special subject of study in national school curricula. Its purpose should be to promote greater understanding of international institutions, of humanitarian issues and human rights, and to stress the need for a multilateral and multicultural approach to global problems. At the same time, in view of the importance of developing greater understanding between peoples, we believe that international organizations and governments should support the **exchange among countries** of scholars, professionals, artists and others. In particular, we wish to encourage countries of the South to increase such exchanges of such people among themselves.

* The importance of the media in influencing policies cannot be over-emphasized. We urge them to include humanitarian issues as an important part of their activities. Newspapers as well as television and radio programmes should carry special sections devoted to these issues. In practical terms, we recommend allocations by the media of more human and financial resources to humanitarian issues. Public media networks should have on their executive boards one or more members chosen for demonstrated commitment to or expertise in humanitarian affairs.

* The non-governmental organizations, (NGOs) have a particularly important role to play in the promotion of humanitarian issues and in filling the gaps that exist in the international policies and actions. We commend them for the valuable role they play, particularly at the grassroots level, and urge them to intensify further the activities which contribute to raising public awareness of humanitarian issues and to encouraging action. NGOs are often the voice of the powerless as well as an expression of world public opinion. Their strength lies in their diversity and their concentration on single issues. We note with satisfaction their growth in size, income and influence in recent years. We are convinced of the need to develop strong and effective NGOs in the South. The more affluent NGOs of the North can and should play a more vigorous role in this regard. Likewise, there is a need, in our view, for more efficient networking and co-ordination of activities both in sectoral and geographic terms. Co-operation within and among countries through NGO networks at regional and international level can be a vital factor for the promotion and strengthening of multilateralism as well as international understanding.

* In the general context of NGO work, we also recommend that the young develop more effective lobbying organizations. We

believe that they should be granted a greater say in local, national and international affairs because of their numerical importance and because of their vigour, optimism and longer time perspective. We recommend that children's organizations, both governmental and non-governmental, develop a real dialogue between young people and the international organizations with a view to promoting their rights and improving their conditions. Consultations to this end should take place on a regular basis, in different regions, and efforts should be made to involve young people outside the mainstream.

★ Finally, we emphasize the need to build upon the existing structure of human rights and humanitarian principles by identifying and promoting those human values and norms which are common to all cultures and creeds in all continents. It will be appropriate in celebrating, in 1988, the fortieth anniversary of the Universal Declaration of Human Rights, to begin a new process which, while strengthening the existing instruments, looks to the future in the light of primary considerations to which we referred at the beginning of this Report, such as respect for life, inter-generational responsibility, protection of the human habitat and altruism.

In concluding this Report, we wish to reaffirm our faith in the ability of humankind to overcome the colossal challenges facing it. Our plea for progress in the humanitarian field is not intended to downplay the need for progress in other areas – economic, political and global security. Indeed, we recognize that progress in these fields is essential for promoting the causes we espouse. But somehow, somewhere, the vicious circle of confrontation and conflict has to be broken. We believe humanitarianism can and must play that role. In our view, it is a field in which ideological differences, North–South problems and East–West rivalries can be transcended. The recognition of the fundamental worth of the human person and the ethical values shared by all societies must be the sustaining force behind common action for common good.

Annex I

United Nations General Assembly

Forty-second session : 1987
Agenda Item 106: New International Humanitarian Order

Resolution Adopted Without a Vote by the General Assembly
(9 December 1987)

(Resolution introduced by Jordan and co-sponsored by Algeria, Australia, Austria, Bahrain, Bangladesh, Cameroon, Canada, Colombia, Costa Rica, Democratic Yemen, Djibouti, Egypt, France, Greece, Indonesia, Iraq, Italy, Jamaica, Japan, Kuwait, Lebanon, the Libyan Arab Jamahiriya, Mauritania, Morocco, Oman, Pakistan, the Philippines, Qatar, Romania, Samoa, Saudi Arabia, Senegal, Somalia, Sri Lanka, the Sudan, the United Arab Emirates, the United Republic of Tanzania, Yemen and Yugoslavia.).

The General Assembly,

Recalling its resolutions 36/136 of 14 December 1981, 37/201 of 18 December 1982, 38/125 of 16 December 1983 and 40/126 of 13 December 1985,
Recalling further the reports of the Secretary-General,*
Bearing in mind the comments communicated by Governments to the Secretary-General regarding a New International Humanitarian Order,

---

* A/37/145, A/38/450, A/40/348 and Add. 1 and 2, A/41/472.

Recognizing the urgent need further to improve and strengthen the international framework relating to humanitarian issues, while taking fully into account existing instruments and mechanisms,

Noting with concern that emergencies and disasters, mostly man-made, have increased in frequency in recent years, posing a growing challenge to mechanisms of international responses to them,

Aware that institutional arrangements and actions of governmental and non-governmental bodies require further invigoration as well as adjustment to new realities in order to respond more effectively and speedily to contemporary humanitarian problems,

Noting the efforts of the Independent Commission on International Humanitarian Issues to promote public awareness of humanitarian issues, analyse relatively neglected aspects and identify alternative approaches for resolving humanitarian problems,

Noting further the establishment, outside the United Nations, of an Independent Bureau for Humanitarian Issues to disseminate and follow up on the work of the Independent Commission,

Taking note of the Report of the Independent Commission, as well as the sectoral reports on specific humanitarian issues:

1. **Expresses its appreciation** to the co-chairmen and members of the Independent Commission on International Humanitarian Issues for their humanitarian endeavours;

2. **Draws the attention** of Governments as well as inter-governmental organizations, including those functioning at the regional level, to the Report of the Independent Commission;

3. **Requests** the Independent Commission to transmit its Report to Member States as well as to the executive heads of specialized agencies and programmes of the United Nations system in order to enable them to consider its analyses and conclusions;

4. **Invites** all non-governmental organizations concerned with the humanitarian issues examined by the Independent Commission to bear in mind the recommendations and suggestions made in its Report in the context of their policies and actions in the field;

5. **Invites** Governments to make available to the Secretary-General, on a voluntary basis, information and expertise on humanitarian issues of concern to them, in order to identify opportunities for future action and to strengthen international co-operation in the humanitarian field;

6. **Requests** the Secretary-General to remain in contact with Governments, relevant specialized agencies and programmes of the United Nations system, non-governmental organizations concerned as well as the Independent Bureau for Humanitarian Issues and to report, on the basis of information made available to him, on the progress

made in the humanitarian field to the General Asssembly at its forty-third session;

7. **Decides** to review at its forty-third session the question of a New International Humanitarian Order.

Annex II

ICIHI PUBLICATIONS

Sectoral Reports

(List of editions/languages not exhaustive)

Famine: A Man-Made Disaster?
(Pan Books, London/Sydney, 1985: British Edition)
Famine: A Man-Made Disaster?
(Random House, New York, 1985: American Edition)
Famine: A Man-Made Disaster?
(Sekai No Ugoki Sha, Tokyo, 1985: Japanese Edition)
Fame: Un disastro creato dall'uomo?
(Tascabili Bompiani, Milan, 1985: Italian Edition)
Glad: Udeo ljudi u ovoj katastrofi?
(Medunarodna politika, Belgrade, 1985: Serbo-Croatian Edition)
La Famine: Mieux comprendre, mieux aider
(Berger-Levrault, Paris, 1985: French Edition)
Fome: Catastrofe provocada pelo homem?
Editora Vozes, Petropolis, Rio de Janeiro, 1986: Brazilian Edition)
El Hombre – Una tragedia evitable
(Alianza Editorial, Madrid, 1986: Spanish Edition)
Almaja'a: Karita Min Sani Al Insan?
(Al Ahram, Cairo, 1986: Arabic Edition)

Editions to appear later: Bulgarian, Russian.

* * *

Winning the Human Race?

The Encroaching Desert: The Consequences of Human Failure
(Zed Books, London/New Jersey, 1986; College Press, Harare, 1986:
English Edition)
La Désertification
(Berger-Levrault, Paris, 1986: French Edition)
Altasahor
Al Ahram, Cairo, 1986: Arabic Edition)
The Encroaching Desert: The Consequences of Human Failure
(Chinese Academy of Sciences, Beijing, 1988: Chinese Edition)
The Encroaching Desert: The Consequences of Human Failure
(ARENA Press, Hong Kong, 1988: Asia and Pacific Edition)

Editions to appear later: Russian, Spanish.

*   *   *

The Vanishing Forest: The Human Consequences of Deforestation
(Zed Books, London/New Jersey, 1986; College Press, Harare, 1986;
Sun Book Co., Kuala Lumpur, Malaysia, 1987)
La Déforestation: Aspects humanitaires
(Berger-Levrault, Paris, 1986: French Edition)
Nestajanje Suma: Posledice Na Ljudski Rod
(Medunarodna politika, Belgrade, 1986: Serbo-Croatian Edition)
The Vanishing Forest: The Human Consequences of Deforestation
(International Relations Publishing House, Moscow, 1987: Russian
Edition)
The Vanishing Forest: The Human Consequences of Deforestation
(Chinese Academy of Sciences, Beijing, 1988: Chinese Edition)
The Vanishing Forest: The Human Consequences of Deforestation
(ARENA Press, Hong Kong 1988: Asia and Pacific Edition)

Editions to appear later: Indonesian, Spanish.

*   *   *

Street Children: A Growing Urban Tragedy
(Weidenfeld & Nicolson, London, 1986: British Edition)
Les enfants de la rue: L'autre visage de la ville
(Berger-Levrault, Paris, 1986: French Edition)
Atfal Al Shawar'ih: Masa'at Hadariyat Moutanamiyat
(Arab Thought Forum, Amman, 1987: Arabic Edition)
Deca Ulice: Rastuca Gradska Tragedija
(Medunarodna politika, Belgrade, 1986: Serbo-Croatian Edition)
I Ragazzi della Strada : l'Altra Faccia della Citta

204

Tascabili Bompiani, Milan, 1987: Italian Edition)

Editions to appear later: Indonesian, Japanese, and Spanish.

* * *

Modern Wars: The Humanitarian Challenge
(Zed Books, London/New Jersey, 1986: British Edition)
La Guerre Aujourd'hui: défi humanitaire
(Berger-Levrault, Paris, 1986: French Edition)

Editions to appear later: Japanese, Russian and Spanish.

* * *

Disappeared! Technique of Terror
(Zed Books, London/New Jersey, 1986: British Edition)
Disparus: Pourquoi?
(Berger-Levrault, Paris, 1986: French Edition)
Disappeared! Technique of Terror
(International Relations Publishing House, 1987: Russian Edition)
Disappeared! Technique of Terror
(ARENA Press, Hong Kong, 1988: Asia and Pacific Edition)

Editions to appear later: Indonesian, Portuguese and Spanish.

* * *

Refugees: Dynamics of Displacement
(Zed Books, London/New Jersey, 1986: British Edition)
Réfugiés: La dynamique du déplacement
(Berger-Levrault, Paris, 1988: French Edition)
Refugees: Dynamics of Displacement
(International Relations Publishing House, Moscow, 1987: Russian Edition)
Refugees: Dynamics of Displacement
(ARENA Press, Hong Kong, 1988: Asia and Pacific Edition)

Editions to appear later: Arabic, Indonesian, Japanese, Spanish and Thai.

* * *

Indigenous Peoples
(Zed Books, London/New Jersey, 1987: British Edition)

Winning the Human Race?

Les peuples autochtones
(Berger-Levrault, Paris, 1988: French Edition)

Editions to appear later: Bengali, Hindi, Japanese, Portuguese, Quechua, Russian and Spanish.

Other reports prepared in conjunction with ICIHI:

Protection of Children: Proceedings of Amman Symposium
(ICIHI, Geneva, 1986: English Edition)
Rehabilitation of Degraded Tropical Rainforest Lands
(International Union for Conservation of Nature and Natural Resources, Gland, 1985)
Economic Use of Tropical Moist Forests
(IUCN Commission on Ecology, Gland, 1985)
The Future of Tropical Rain Forests in South East Asia
(IUCN Commission on Ecology, Gland, 1985)
Proceedings of The Tokyo Forum: Ethics of Human Survival
(National Institute for Research Advancement, Tokyo, 1985)

Other sectoral reports to be published include:

- *People Without a Country: The Problem of Statelessness*
- *The Scape-Goats: Victims of Mass Expulsions*
- *Disaster Management*
- *The Protection of Children: A Task for Our Times*
- *Urban Outcasts: Young People in the Cities*
- *Modern Disasters: The Human Consequences of New Technology*
- *The Uprooted: Specific Aspects of The Refugee Problem*
- *First Nations: Problems of Indigenous Peoples*

ICIHI TV Programmes

The Independent Commission decided at the outset that in order to reach and influence a wide public around the world, it would be necessary to use the media, particularly television. A series of eight short TV programmes entitled *Humanitas*, destined essentially for

Third World TV networks, has been designed to cover some selected humanitarian issues. The Commission is providing these films as support material to its reports and recommendations. The first six of the following films have been completed.

1. *Bitter Harvests* (TV Documentary : 25 minutes). The story of continuing desertification in developed and developing countries.

2. *Vanishing Forests* (TV Documentary : 25 minutes). The problem of deforestation, its consequences and impact on human-beings.

3. *Street Children* (TV Documentary : 25 minutes). A global view of the problem of abandoned and alienated children both in the rich and poor countries of the world: how they survive and what can be done to help them.

4. *Indigenous Peoples* (TV Documentary : 45 minutes). Relating to the problems faced by some 200 million indigenous peoples, particularly in Asia and Latin America – ethnocide perpetrated against them and the flagrant discrimination by dominant societies of which they continue to be victims.

5. *Disappeared Persons* (TV Documentary : 25 minutes). The story of kidnapping, torture and murder carried out on behalf of governments. The practice of 'disappearances' is not limited just to Latin American countries but is spread around the world : 40 countries are known to have had recourse to it, according to the UN.

6. *Refugees* (TV Documentary : 20 minutes). A global view of the problem of forced displacement and uprootedness. The film deals with the increasingly serious problem of some 15 million refugees, affecting all parts of the world.

7. *Armed Conflicts* (TV Documentary : 30 minutes). Few people realize that, since World War II, 20 million people have died in local wars. More than thirty armed conflicts are raging around the world right now. This documentary deals with the continuing problem of armed conflicts and the violation of humanitarian norms.

8. *Disasters and Disaster Management* (TV Documentary : 35 minutes). Despite modern technological progress, the number of disasters and the victims they claim has been increasing during recent years. Why? And what can be done about it? The documentary also deals with relatively new man-made catastrophes, e.g. industrial and nuclear accidents.

Annex III

INFORMATION NOTE ON THE INDEPENDENT COMMISSION ON INTERNATIONAL HUMANITARIAN ISSUES

The establishment of an Independent Commission on International Humanitarian Issues (ICIHI) was the response of a group of eminent persons from all parts of the world to the deeply felt need to enhance public awareness of important humanitarian issues and to promote an international climate favouring progress in the humanitarian field.

The work of the Commission was intended to be a part of the continuing search of the world community for a more adequate international framework to uphold human dignity and rise to the challenge of colossal humanitarian problems arising with increasing frequency in all continents.

In 1981, the United Nations General Assembly adopted by consensus a resolution relating to a New International Humanitarian Order in which it recognized: "The importance of further improving a comprehensive international framework which takes fully into account existing instruments relating to humanitarian questions as well as the need for addressing those aspects which are not yet adequately covered." In doing so, the Assembly bore in mind that "institutional arrangements and actions of governmental and non-governmental bodies might need to be further strengthened to respond effectively in situations requiring humanitarian action." (A/36/136)

The following year, the General Assembly adopted a further resolution relating to the New International Humanitarian Order in which it noted "the proposal for establishment, outside the United Nations framework, of an Independent Commission on International Humanitarian Issues composed of leading personalities in the humanitarian field or having wide experience of government or world affairs." (A/37/201)

The Independent Commission on International Humanitarian Issues was established in 1983 and held its first plenary meeting in New York in November that year. A few days later, the UN General Assembly adopted another resolution in which it noted the establishment of the Commission and requested the Secretary-General to remain in contact with governments as well as the Independent Commission in order to provide a comprehensive report on the subject to the Assembly. (A/38/125)

In 1985, the Secretary-General presented to the General Assembly his report as well as comments from governments on the New International Humanitarian Order. The report included a description of the Independent Commission and its work. In a subsequent resolution, the General Assembly took note of the activities of the Commission and looked forward to the outcome of its efforts and its Final Report. (A/40/126)

In December 1987, the General Assembly adopted without a vote a further resolution (A/42/120) relating to the work of the Independent Commission on the basis of the present Report. The full text of this resolution which provides insights into the thinking of governments and the latest position regarding the ICIHI and its follow-up mechanism is provided as Annex I of this book.

Composition of the Commission

The Commission was an independent body whose members participated in their personal capacity and not as representatives of governments or international bodies to which they might have belonged. Its work was not intended to interfere with governmental negotiations or inter-state relations, nor to duplicate work being done by existing governmental or non-governmental bodies.

In its deliberations the Commission benefited from the advice of governments, existing international governmental and non-governmental bodies and leading experts. The composition of the Commission was limited and based on equitable geographical distribution. It had twenty-nine members. Details regarding the members are to be found at the end of this Note.

The Purpose of the Commission
The purpose of the Commission was:
* To study specific humanitarian issues that have been inadequately dealt with to date, or call for solutions in line with new realities;

209

* ★ To identify opportunities for more effective action by the international community and to make practical, action-oriented proposals that promote the well-being of people;

* ★ To enhance public awareness of the conditions that create and perpetuate human suffering, and to strengthen efforts, at governmental and non-governmental level to bring about changes that will help make the world a more humane place.

The Work of the Commission was determined by the desire to be realistic, pragmatic and innovative. During its limited life-span, the Commission focused on three broad areas of concern:

Humanitarian Norms in the context of armed conflicts. Although considerable progress has been made in developing and codifying international humanitarian law, flagrant disregard of humanitarian norms persists. This reality spells heightened dangers for the victims of armed conflicts, an increasing number of whom are civilians. The aim of the Commission, on the one hand, was to encourage actively adhesion by governments to existing international instruments and, on the other, to propose measures that deal with new problems arising out of contemporary armed conflicts.

Disasters, natural and man-made, are not a new phenomenon. But their debilitating frequency and catastrophic consequences provoke pertinent questions as to the international community's ability and willingness to address the root causes of such calamities. The new humanitarian crises demonstrate the necessity of new perspectives and approaches in translating the short-term relief efforts of today into long-term strategies that safeguard the welfare of future generations. The factors which create disasters – and most cannot simply be attributed to the caprices of nature – are many and complex. The Commission, therefore, selected a number of inter-related issues that are central to disaster prevention and preparedness. Particularly concerned about the destruction of the earth's resources, the Commission focused on the humanitarian aspects of problems such as desertification, deforestation, famine as well as such man-made disasters as nuclear and industrial accidents.

Vulnerable Groups is a term attributed to many who suffer deprivation by virtue of their status in society. However, given that the Commission's work was limited in time and scope, it concentrated on the plight of only a few of the unprotected or vulnerable groups in specific situations of acute hardship. These include the stateless, the

210

disappeared, refugees and displaced persons, indigenous populations, street children and the urban young. The Commission's purpose was to study the problems unique to each group, the deprivation entailed, the lack of an adequate international response, and the practical measures which could be taken to lessen their hardship.

In addition to analysing and making recommendations on specific issues, sensitizing public opinion, and reminding governments of their humanitarian obligations, the Commission has prepared this Final Report. It reflects the views of its members expressed during eight plenary sessions held in Geneva, New York, Tunis, The Hague, Tokyo, Vienna, Stockholm and Amman, as well as in a number of Working Group meetings organized for in-depth discussions on specific issues. The Final Report has been released with the general approval of all Commissioners. Endorsement of each statement and proposal was, however, not sought on an individual basis. It is issued in the belief that it will facilitate international discussion and action without delay.

The Commission operated through a small secretariat in Geneva which co-ordinated research activities and serviced the work of the Commission. The reports on specific topics addressed by the Commission were formulated after in-depth study by the Commission Members. Working Groups, composed of Members with special interest or expertise in the subject, assisted by a group of recognized experts, were established to investigate different issues. The Working Groups collaborated closely through the secretariat with the relevant academic centres as well as governmental and non-governmental international bodies. Experts as well as representatives of the international bodies concerned were also invited, as appropriate, to participate in the deliberations of the Commission or the Working Groups.

This process ensured that the Commission's activities did not duplicate the work of other organizations but rather complemented the on-going search for better and more effective solutions to humanitarian problems. Draft reports were then reviewed by all the Commission Members. When finalized, they were made public as Sectoral Reports prepared for the Commission.

Periodically, the Commission organized seminars, expert consultations, brain-storming sessions and public meetings to examine issues or to make its views known. This process also promoted a greater awareness and understanding of humanitarian questions.

The work of the Commission was funded by government contributions as well as non-governmental organizations and private sources.

Members of the Commission

Sadruddin AGA KHAN (Iran): UN High Commissioner for Refugees, 1965–77. Special Consultant to the UN Secretary-General since 1978. Special Rapporteur of the UN Human Rights Commission, 1981. Founder-President of the Bellerive Group.

Susanna AGNELLI (Italy): Under-Secretary of State for Foreign Affairs since 1983. Member of the Italian Senate. Member of the European Parliament, 1979–81. Journalist and author.

Talal Bin Abdul Aziz AL SAUD (Saudi Arabia): President, the Arab Gulf Programme for UN Development Organizations (AGFUND). UNICEF's Special Envoy, 1980–84. Former Minister of Communications, of Finance and National Economy and Vice-President of the Supreme Planning Commission.

Paulo Evaristo ARNS (Brazil): Cardinal, Archbishop of Sao Paulo. Chancellor of the Pontifical Catholic University, Sao Paulo State. Author.

Mohammed BEDJAOUI (Algeria): Judge at the International Court of Justice since 1982. Minister of Justice, 1964–70. Ambassador to France, 1970–79; UNESCO, 1971–79; and the United Nations in New York, 1979–82. Author.

Henrik BEER (Sweden): Secretary-General of the League of Red Cross Societies, 1960–82. Secretary-General of the Swedish Red Cross, 1947–60. Member of the International Institute for Environment and Development and the International Institute of Humanitarian Law (Deceased 1987).

Igor P. BLISHCHENKO (USSR): Professor of Legal Sciences, Chairman of the International Law Department, Moscow. Member of Soviet delegations to international humanitarian meetings, including the Diplomatic Conference on the Reaffirmation and Development of International Humanitarian Law. Consultant to the Soviet Academy of Sciences.

Luis ECHEVERRIA ALVAREZ (Mexico): President of the Republic, 1970–76. Founder and Director-General of the Centre for Economic and Social Studies of the Third World, 1976. Former Ambassador to Australia, New Zealand and UNESCO.

Pierre GRABER (Switzerland): President of the Swiss Confederation, 1975. Foreign Minister, 1975–78. President of the Diplomatic Conference on the Reaffirmation and Development of International Humanitarian Law, 1974–77.

Ivan L. HEAD (Canada): President of the International Development Research Centre (IDRC). Special Assistant to the Prime Minister of Canada, 1968–78. Queen's Counsel.

M. HIDAYATULLAH (India): Vice-President of India, 1979–84. Former Chief Justice of the Supreme Court. Chancellor of the Jamia Millia Islamia since 1979. Former Chancellor of the Universities of Delhi, Punjab. Author.

Aziza HUSSEIN (Egypt): Member of the Population Council. President of the International Planned Parenthood Federation, 1977–85. Fellow of the International Peace Academy, Helsinki, 1971 and the Aspen Institute of Humanistic Studies, 1978–79.

Manfred LACHS (Poland): Judge at the International Court of Justice since 1967 and its President, 1973–76. Professor of Political Science and International Law. Former Chairman of the UN Legal Committee on the Peaceful Uses of Outer Space. Author.

Robert S. McNAMARA (USA): President of the World Bank, 1968–81. Secretary of Defense, 1961–68. President, Ford Motor Company, 1960–61. Trustee of the Brookings Institute, Ford Foundation, the Urban Institute and the California Institute of Technology. Author.

Lazar MOJSOV (Yugoslavia): President of the Presidency of the Socialist Federal Republic of Yugoslavia. Former Foreign Minister. Ambassador to the USSR, Mongolia, Austria, the United Nations, 1958–74. President of the UN General Assembly, 32nd Session and of the Special Session on Disarmament, 1978.

Mohamed MZALI (Tunisia): Former Prime Minister and General Secretary of the Destorian Socialist Party. Former Minister of National Defence, Education, Youth and Sports and Health. Author.

Sadako OGATA (Japan): Professor at the Institute of International Relations, Sophia University, Tokyo. Representative of Japan to the United Nations Human Rights Commission. Member of the Trilateral Commission.

213

David OWEN (United Kingdom): Member of Parliament since 1966. Leader of the Social Democratic Party since 1983. Foreign Secretary, 1977–79.

Willibald P. PAHR (Austria): Secretary-General of the World Tourism Organization, Madrid. Federal Minister of Foreign Affairs, 1976–83. Ambassador. Vice-President of the International Institute of Human Rights, Strasbourg.

Shridath S. RAMPHAL (Guyana): Secretary-General of the Commonwealth since 1975. Former Attorney-General, Foreign Minister and Minister of Justice.

RU XIN (China): Vice-President of the Chinese Academy of Social Sciences. Professor of Philosophy at the Xiamen University. Executive President of the Chinese National Society of the History of World Philosophies.

Salim A. SALIM (Tanzania): Deputy Prime Minister and Minister of Defence. Former Prime Minister and Foreign Minister. Ambassador to Egypt, India, China and Permanent Representative to the United Nations. Former President of the UN General Assembly and the Security Council.

Léopold Sédar SENGHOR (Senegal): Member of the French Academy. President of the Republic of Senegal, 1960–80. Cabinet Minister in the French Government before leading his country to independence in 1960. Poet and philosopher.

SOEDJATMOKO (Indonesia): Former Rector of the United Nations University, Tokyo, 1980–87. Ambassador to the United States. Member of the Club of Rome and Trustee of the Aspen Institute and the Ford Foundation. Author.

Hassan bin TALAL (Jordan): Crown Prince of the Hashemite Kingdom. Founder of the Royal Scientific Society and the Arab Thought Forum. Concerned with development planning of Jordan and the formulation of national, economic and social policies. Author.

Desmond TUTU (South Africa): Archbishop of Cape Town. Winner of Nobel Peace Prize. Former Secretary-General of the South African Council of Churches. Professor of Theology.

Simone VEIL (France): Member of the European Parliament and its

President 1979–82. Chairperson of the Legal Affairs Committee of the European Parliament. Former Minister of Health, Social Security and Family Affairs, 1974–79.

E. Gough WHITLAM (Australia): Former Prime Minister, 1972–75. Member of Parliament, 1952–78. Former Minister of Foreign Affairs and Ambassador to UNESCO.

Just as the final report was being finalized, Mr Henrik Beer (Sweden) passed away. He was the Commission's Treasurer as well as Chairman of its Working Group on Disasters. Mr Adam Malik (Indonesia) who joined the Commission at its inception was able to attend only two meetings before his untimely demise. The Commission records its sense of loss as well as its deepest appreciation for their dedicated service.

*   *   *

Secretariat of the Commission

The Swiss Government facilitated the establishment of the Secretariat in Geneva in proximity to the numerous international humanitarian organizations functioning there. The staff was recruited on a short-term basis and rotated according to the exigencies of the Commission's programme of work but remained very small, consisting of a handful of professional and support staff. Zia Rizvi, a senior United Nations official was detached to the Commission for the total period of its activity. He directed the Secretariat and assumed responsibility for editing this Report and the various sectoral reports published under the aegis of the Commission. Brian Walker served as the Director until December 1985. Jean-Bernard Ducrest, Maria de Sousa and Michel Vieux helped in the administrative arrangements.

For varying periods of time, the following worked as support staff in the Secretariat: Bettina Balmer, Monique Fritsch, Maeve Fitzgerald, Fiona Frank, Liliane de Giorgi, Martine Jacometti, Camille Kryspin, Marie-José Louis and Anne Toh. Research assistance and advice was provided at various times by Rosemary Abi-Saab, Paolo Bifani, Pierre Bringuier, Dee Ann Caflisch, Nigel Cantwell, Jumphot Chuasai, Padraig Czajkowski, Jeff Crisp, Richard Falk, Merrick Fall, Victor-Yves Ghebali, Nick de Keller, Joan Mahalic, Norah Niland, Roxanne Dunbar Ortiz, Anita Singh, Bernarda Smit, Isabelle Subirats, Darka Topali, Etse Wolde-Giyorgis, Minja Yang and Sharareh Zolfagari.

Much of the substantive work on this Report and the various

sectoral reports was done by Julian Berger, Mohamed El-Kouhene, Drew Mahalic and Pierre Spitz.

To all these staff members and many others who helped, the Commission records its deep appreciation. They laboured under pressure to meet the demands of a heavy workload and often went beyond the call of duty to service diligently the meetings of the Commission and its working groups.

Valuable support was provided to the ICIHI Secretariat by some of the staff colleagues of individual Commissioners. The assistance of Ms Kathleen Newland of the United Nations University, Tokyo, and of Hugh Craft, Clive Jordan and Pera Wells of the Commonwealth Secretariat, London, is gratefully acknowledged. Thanks are due also to Michael Keating, Shehab Madi, Filippo di Robilant and Margaret Smart.

Plenary Meetings of the Commission

The Commission was inaugurated in Geneva at the Palais des Nations, in the presence of the UN Secretary-General, in July 1983. Statements were made by Crown Prince Hassan bin Talal, Prince Sadruddin Aga Khan, Mr Perez de Cuellar, and Mr Probst representing the host Government. A special message was received from His Holiness the Pope John-Paul II. The Commission was received by the President of Switzerland and met senior Swiss and UN officials as well as permanent representatives accredited to the United Nations. After the inauguration, the Commission met briefly at the Institut Henri Dunant to discuss its programme of work. It decided to hold its first plenary meeting in New York. It also heard statements by Sir Robert Jackson on disaster management and by Ms Julia Taft on humanitarian norms in armed conflicts.

The first plenary meeting of the Commission was held in New York in November 1983. It discussed the preliminary papers submitted to it on the three areas it decided to study: humanitarian norms in armed conflicts, man-made disasters and vulnerable groups. The following appeared before the Commission and made substantive statements: Mr Alexandre Haye, President of the International Committee of the Red Cross (ICRC), on humanitarian norms in armed conflicts; Mr M'hamed Essaafi, UN Under Secretary-General and head of the UN Disaster Relief Office (UNDRO); Mr Jean-Pierre Hocké, then Director of Operations of ICRC and now UN High Commissioner for Refugees and Mr Anders Wijkman, Secretary-General of the Swedish Red Cross, on various aspects of disaster management; Mr Hipolito

Solari Yrigoyen, Mrs Marta Casal de Gatti and Mr Julio Cortazar, as well as representatives of the Grandmothers of the Plaza de Mayo, Buenos Aires, on the subject of 'disappearances'. The Commission established various working groups to examine the specific issues selected by it for in-depth study. Commissioners also met the UN Secretary-General, senior UN officials and various ambassadors.

The second plenary meeting was held in Hammamet, Tunisia, in May 1984. The meeting paid special attention to the dramatic situation prevailing in Africa at that time and issued a substantive public statement containing a series of recommendations relating to short and long-term measures that could be taken to address the problem of famine. The Commission also heard statements by Mr Joseph Wheeler, Deputy Executive Director of the UN Environment Programme (UNEP), and Mr Mansour Khalid, Vice-Chairman of the World Commission on Environment and Development (WCED). The Commission met the President of the Republic of Tunisia and senior officials of the Government.

The third plenary meeting was held at the Peace Palace, The Hague, Netherlands, in December 1984. The Commission reviewed the work done by its working groups on famine, desertification, deforestation, and early-warning systems. It also held a special session devoted to the problems of the young, attended by Her Majesty the Queen of the Netherlands and Prince Klaus. The Commission decided to address a detailed memorandum to all Governments which had not adhered to the 1977 Geneva Protocols relating to humanitarian norms in armed conflicts. The Commission also heard statements by Mr Michael Mann, Dean of Windsor, Professor Draper, University of Sussex, and Professor Gordenker, University of Princeton. The Commission was received by H. M. Queen Beatrix and met with senior Dutch officials, judges of the International Court of Justice and representatives of Dutch non-governmental organizations.

The fourth plenary meeting was held at the United Nations University in Tokyo, Japan, in June 1985. It was devoted essentially to the consideration of various vulnerable groups. Special attention was paid to the problems of refugees and displaced persons as well as indigenous peoples. The Commission also considered the conceptual framework of its final report and took note of the publication of the first book (on famine) in its series of sectoral reports. Substantive statements were made by Ambassador Korino who headed the Japanese team of experts working on the refugee problem for the Commission, as well as Professor Onishi of Soka University. The Commission also held a one-day public meeting in collaboration with the National Institute for Research Advancement of Japan (NIRA) and the United Nations University. The statements made by the

Commission members and eminent Japanese experts as well as a summary of the public debate that followed were later published by NIRA in English and Japanese in a booklet entitled *Ethics of Human Survival*. Private meetings were held with the Prime Minister and eminent persons in Japan.

The fifth plenary meeting was held in Vienna, Austria, in December 1985. It noted the publication of the sectoral reports on desertification and deforestation which followed the book on famine. The Commission also examined the working group reports on street children, disappearances and refugees. Substantive statements were made by Mr Kurt Herndl, Assistant Secretary-General and Director of the UN Centre for Human Rights, Mr Ivan Tosevski, Chairman of the UN Working Group on Disappearances, and Mr G. Mauntner-Markhof of the UN Secretariat. In addition, the Nobel Laureate, Professor Abdus Salam, appeared before the Commission in connection with the problem of communal riots. The Commission also held a public meeting at the Hofburg Palace in collaboration with the Austrian Institute of International Affairs. Commissioners met the President of the Republic and senior officials of the Government.

The sixth plenary meeting was held in Stockholm, Sweden, in May 1986, in the wake of the nuclear accident at Chernobyl. The Commission discussed the future of commercial nuclear power as well as the problem of weapons of mass destruction. A communiqué containing the Commission's recommendations regarding these questions was issued. The Commission also examined its draft final report. It heard statements by Mr Jozef Goldblat of the Swedish Institute for Peace Research (SIPRI) and Mr Jacques Moreillon, Director-General of ICRC, on issues relating to armed conflicts. A public meeting devoted to different aspects of the increasing use of violence was held in collaboration with the Swedish Institute for International Relations. The Commission also met the Prime Minister and other senior officials of the Swedish Government.

The seventh and last plenary meeting of the Commission was held in Amman, Jordan, in December 1986. This meeting was devoted entirely to the draft final report of the Commission. The Commission took note of the publication of sectoral reports on disappearances, street children, refugees and modern wars, and examined the draft framework of the report on indigenous peoples. It also finalized arrangements regarding the completion of its series of sectoral reports and the follow-up mechanism, as well as action to be taken within the UN system. The Commission met His Majesty King Hussein as well as the Prime Minister and other senior officials of the Government.

All the meetings of the various working groups taking place between plenary sessions were held at the ICIHI Secretariat with the exception of one on indigenous peoples which was held in Strasbourg. In many cases, the occasion of the plenary meetings was also used to hold meetings of working groups before or after them. Details regarding attendance are contained in the sectoral reports enumerated in Annex II of this book. The Commission records its appreciation to all the experts and eminent persons who appeared before it and made valuable contributions to its deliberations.

Financial Contributions

The Government of Switzerland provided the premises and logistical support to the Secretariat of the Commission. It also granted diplomatic privileges and immunities to the members of the Commission and the Secretariat. In addition, the following Governments made financial contributions: Canada, Cyprus, Denmark, Egypt, Finland, Japan, Kuwait, Pakistan, Sweden, Tunisia, U.S.A. as well as the European Economic Community. The Governments of Austria, Japan, Jordan, Sweden and Tunisia also contributed towards the costs of the plenary meetings of the Commission held in those countries.

The following non-governmental organizations also made financial contributions: CEBEMO (Holland), Japan Shipbuilding Foundation (Japan), Oxfam (U.K.), Radda Barnen (Sweden) and Soka Gakkai (Japan).

Approximately half the expenses of the Commission were covered through contributions from private sources. Contributions were made by the following: Prince Talal bin Abdul Aziz Al Saud, Sheikh Khalifa Bin Hamad Al-Thani, Prince Karim Aga Khan, Prince Sadruddin Aga Khan, Crown Prince Hassan bin Talal, Zia Rizvi and Abbas Gokal.

The Commission expresses its deepest gratitude and sincere appreciation to these Governments, non-governmental organizations and individuals for their valuable support to its work.

The accounts of the Commission were audited by Klynveld Main Goerdeler International (KMG, a member of the Chambre Suisse des sociétés fiduciaires et des experts-comptables).

Acknowledgements

The Commission is grateful for the expert advice and valuable assistance provided by a great many individuals, including in particular:

Georges Abi-Saab, Nelson O. Addo, Aderanti Adepoju, J. Adomako-Sarfoh, Gudmundur Alfredsson, A. Artucio, Maurice Aubert, Sydney

Bailey, Martin Barber, Amar Bentoumi, Assefa Bequele, Howard Berman, B. Bernus, Geoffrey Best, Maarten Bijleveld, Jo Boyden, Oscar Bremaud, D. Burns, Albert Butros, H. Callaway, G. Campbell, Marta Casal de Gatti, Antonio Cassese, Robert Chambers, Azam Chaudhry, Kraisak Choonhavan, B. Clark, R. Clarke, Judith Clopeau, Marcus Colchester, Gervais Coles, Luigi Condorelli, Steven Corry, Julio Cortazar, Bruce Currey, Peter Cutler, Erika-Irene Daes, Harry W. Daniels, Maureen Davis, J. Derclayes, C. Desormeaux, Leandro Despouy, Didier Laurent, Karl Doehring, Ustinia Dolgopol, Clermonde Dominicé, G. D. Draper, Krzysztof Drzewicki, Frances D'Souza, André Dunant, Jan Egeland, Charles Egger, Asbjorn Eide, Simone Ek, Farouk ElBaz, Judith Ennew, M'hamed Essaafi, M. Esnard, Cliff Everest, Peter Farago, Florentino Feliciano, L. Filippi-Wilhelm, J. Forbes, David Forsythe, Robert Freedman, Alec Fyfe, J. G. Galaty, Dennis Gallager, Hans-Peter Gasser, G. Gatti, Kate George, Susan George, Jozef Goldblat, Guy Goodwin-Gill, Leon Gordenker, B. Graefrath, John Gray, Nahla Haider, Barbara Harrell-Bond, Michael Harris, Richard Hauser, Julia Hausermann, Alexandre Hay, Roger Hay, Kurt Herndl, D. Hidalgo Schnur, Jean-Pierre Hocké, C. Hogg, Gilbert Jaeger, Harriet Jakobsson, Basharat Jazbi, Louis Joinet, Elimane Kane, Mohamed Kassas, R. Kawade, Randolph Kent, Mansour Khalid, Isabelle King, Benedict Kingsbury, D. Kintz, Jill Korbin, René Kosirnik, Ohtori Kurino, Y. Lagier, Robert Lamb, Häkan Landelius, Virginia Leary, Thierry Lemaresquier, Patricia Light, Peter Macalister Smith, Hugh McKay, Mark Malloch Brown, Georges Mauntner-Markhof, T. B. Meyer, Dominique Micheli, José Mico, Joseph Moerman, Robert Molteno, Jacques Moreillon, P. Morisson, Audrey Moser, Peter Mutharika, Norman Myers, R. Natkiel, L. Nato, Mildred Neville, D. Ngabonziza, Konstantin Obradovic, Anna Mamalakis Pappas, Roland Pierre Paringaux, Dr Paskins, Margaret Peil, C. Pennati, Sava Penkov, Elvira Perez, Richard Perruchoud, Jean Pictet, David Pitt, Roger Plant, Denise Plattner, Richard Plender, Duncan Poore, Nicole Questiaux, Robert Quinlan, Michel Raffoul, Pam Rajput, J. B. Ramirez, T. Ranger, Everett Ressler, Patricio Rice, John Rivers, Phillip Rudge, Olivier Russbach, Abdus Salam, Yves Sandoz, Dietrich Schindler, Marie-France Schurmann, Amartya Sen, Ralph Smith, Bruno Sorrentino, Rodolfo Stavenhagen, P. Strachan, Zhu Li Sun, Peter Taçon, G. Teunissen, Lloyd Timberlake, Mostafa Tolba, Jiri Toman, Maurice Torelli, Igor Tosevski, David Turton, Julia Taft, Theo van Boven, R. van der Giesen, Nick van Hear, Michel Veuthey, Fernand Vincent, Tarzie Vittachi, Paul Weis, J. Wheeler, Giles Whitcomb, Anders Wijkman, Hipolito Solari Yrigoyen, Alfred de Zayas.

For enquiries or further information
regarding the work of the Commission,
please write to:

Independent Bureau for Humanitarian Issues
P. O. Box 83
1211 Geneva 20
SWITZERLAND